LEARNING FROM THOREAU

John Griswold, *series editor*

Learning from Thoreau

ANDREW MENARD

The University of Georgia Press

Athens

Published by the University of Georgia Press
Athens, Georgia 30602
www.ugapress.org
© 2018 by Andrew Menard
All rights reserved
Designed by Erin Kirk New
Set in Minion Pro
Printed and bound by Thomson-Shore, Inc.

The paper in this book meets the guidelines for permanence
and durability of the Committee on Production Guidelines for
Book Longevity of the Council on Library Resources.

Most University of Georgia Press titles are
available from popular e-book vendors.

Printed in the United States of America

22   21   20   19   18   P   5   4   3   2   1

Library of Congress Cataloging-in-Publication Data

Names: Menard, Andrew, 1948– author.
Title: Learning from Thoreau / Andrew Menard.
Description: Athens : The University of Georgia Press, 2018. |
Includes bibliographical references and index.
Identifiers: LCCN 2018009661| ISBN 9780820353432 (pbk. : alk. paper) |
ISBN 9780820353449 (ebook)
Subjects: LCSH: Thoreau, Henry David, 1817–1862—Influence. |
Thoreau, Henry David, 1817–1862—Appreciation.
Classification: LCC PS3053 .M45 2018 | DDC 818/.309—dc23
LC record available at https://lccn.loc.gov/2018009661

To my father

CONTENTS

ILLUSTRATIONS

LEARNING FROM THOREAU

Introduction

For more than thirty-five years I have been following the beaten-down path that rings Walden Pond, climbing from the sandy shoreline below to the tangential railroad track above, eager to walk my way into the double-edged world of Henry David Thoreau.

Obviously, there's a repetitive, programmatic aspect to these trips that might become tedious after a while. Toeing a path that always begins and ends in the same place only adds to this possibility. But I like how the details and changes in the landscape emerge against a background of apparent sameness year after year, season after season. Standing before a grid of Andy Warhol's soup cans, for instance, I soon shift my gaze from the mechanical similarity of the images to the slight misregisters of color, the wispy imprints of the silk-screen material, the chance effects of the human hand. I revel in the way repetition yields to variety, multiplication to division, likeness to difference. And I feel exactly the same way when walking around the pond or reading Thoreau's thoughts about it. Thoreau always sought the exaggerated variety of nature in the slow regularity of its seasons, and nearly everything he wrote was shaped by this low-profile aesthetic.

Of course, there's nothing unusual about my visits to Walden Pond, even though they're inspired by a man who supposedly exiled himself to the pond for two years and was original enough to write a book that has made its humble scenery worth visiting ever since. On sultry summer days, I usually share the path with dozens of other people, sometimes forced to saunter single file, and even in the dim light of winter there are always a few people, heavily bundled, looking inward to the crystallizing waters. Surely, I'm right to assume that, in one way or another and to one degree or another, we're all trying to find our way back to Thoreau. During the nineteenth century, Americans moving westward often wrote of the joy they felt knowing that someone half a continent away might be contemplating the same star at the same time. Now it's the pond that's an apex—and time, not distance, that triangulates.

Because Thoreau himself probably spent more time monitoring the pond from the direction of his cabin than from any other, that's usually where my compass settles, too—standing quietly on the shoreline of the cove, a few feet away from the path, several hundred feet from the cairn that now rises where the cabin once stood. Sometimes I linger there for minutes on end. Invariably, I lose track of time. Though I'm tempted to say I fall into a reverie, that's not really what happens. Reverie suggests a feeling of being somewhere *else* in space and time, even *lost* in space and time, and I'm far too situated, far too *present* for that. Why would I choose to examine the landscape with my eyes closed? Instead, I associate these moments with a sensation of specific possibility: I wonder if Thoreau saw this, I wonder if he saw that.

I'm willing to admit that these moments might mean I'm chasing a distant horizon or walking a straight line that turns out to be a labyrinth. As much as the beauty of Thoreau's work clarifies *how* he saw the world around him, *what* he saw is more lost to me than ever. *Ars longa, vita brevis*, the saying goes: art endures, life is short. These days the region around Concord is thick with a mixture of pitch pine, hickory, and oak, but in the 1840s and '50s no more than ten percent of the land was forested, and a shaky ten percent at that. When Thoreau referred to the woods of Walden Pond what he meant was wood*lots*, isolated stands of trees preserved for shingles and firewood, not a pristine state of nature. "This winter they are cutting down our woods more seriously than ever," he notes in a journal entry from 1852, "Fair Haven Hill, Walden, Linnæa Borealis Wood, etc., etc. Thank God, they cannot cut down the clouds!"

What's changed for me over the years is the way I perceive the difference between *Walden* and Walden—the difference between what I expect to see because I'm so familiar with the book and what I actually see when I visit the pond itself. If works of art are first seen in reproduction, they tend to create an interval of longing because the original is almost always better. This is even true of Warhol's works, which would seem ideally suited to reproduction. I remember how stunned I felt when I saw the car crash canvases from his *Death and Disaster* series for the first time. They're huge, overwhelming, perfectly scaled for the impact they create firsthand but lack when printed in a magazine or book. I read somewhere that when several Soviet artists in the early '80s were finally allowed to see an "original" Warhol rather than a pirated or smuggled reproduction, they were equally astonished. On the other hand, a work like *Walden* seems to invite a feeling of disappointment. How could the Walden of today ever measure up to the *Walden* of Thoreau's imagination?

Naturally, the pond itself has never been a stable environment. Nor has it gradually morphed from what it was then to what it is now. If Thoreau was outraged at the havoc taking place in his own lifetime, imagine how he would have reacted to what happened in the next few decades. The Fitchburg Railroad is a constant, adjacent figure in *Walden*, from the cheerful sound of the train's sharp, intrusive whistle to the thawing sides of the Deep Cut the company had excavated above the pond, and Thoreau admits, "I usually go to the village along its causeway, and am, as it were, related to society by this link." But four years after he died, the railroad exploited this link by creating an amusement park and picnic area near the pond that became a popular spot for day-trippers eager to salute Thoreau in droves. In 1924, the photographer Herbert Gleason noted that the pond had become such a "community bathtub" that the name "Thoreau's Rest" referred not to a spot like the cove, but to a nearby hot-dog stand. In 1957, the Middlesex County commissioners figured that the bathtub would be even better for the community if the sandy beach were widened and the areas suitable for picnicking and large gatherings were upgraded by chopping down more trees.

Yet, even as the development of Walden seemed to be depreciating the very values Thoreau believed in, *Walden* kept them alive. "He made the whole world interested in his private experiment at Walden Pond," John Burroughs wrote in 1882. Burroughs, a popular naturalist in his day, was just one of many Americans who came to see both themselves and the entire nation reflected in the waters of the pond. Among those who also made their way to the pond were Emma Lazarus, Walt Whitman, and John Muir. While I can't equate these visits—or my own, for that matter—with the sort of medieval pilgrimage in which people crawled for hundreds of miles on their bloody hands and knees hoping for a vision of some sort, I would say that the simple act of adding a stone to the memorial cairn meant that people came to pay homage to the higher laws of *Walden*. What had long been seen as nothing more than a plain, everyday sheet of water was now an incarnation of American liberty and nature. Being such a symbol may have attracted as much greed and speculation over the years as the kind of pushback that eventually made the pond a state reserve, but that's no less true of Frederick Law Olmsted's Central Park or almost any national park. And it shows us that within a decade or two of Thoreau's death, Walden had already become *Walden* once and for all.

My interest in Thoreau began with the essay "Civil Disobedience." Though my opinion of the essay has changed over the years, I still believe it represents a "counter friction," as Thoreau put it, to the perpetual motion of American idealism. The "more perfect and glorious State" he envisions at the end of the essay is not something idyllic or supremely good but a government, and a society, dedicated to becoming *less bad*. Writing during the antebellum period, Thoreau understood that a majority of his fellow citizens believed they were living up to, not betraying, the nation's ideals by returning runaway slaves to their Southern owners, declaring war on Mexico, exterminating Indians, and expanding ever westwards. But he also recognized how loosely these providential ideals were bolted to the machinery of American life and how poorly they engineered a feeling of universal accord. The soldier and politician Sam Houston once said that Americans were so consumed by individualism and self-interest that the United States needed to start a war every decade or two just to renew its shared sense of virtue and purpose. Another way of putting this is that the United States was a nation in which isolation was redeemed by conformity. But "Civil Disobedience" turned this untenable situation upside down, suggesting that individualism ought to be an expression of dissent, not compliance, and that dissent itself was the only legitimate form of idealism and national unity. In place of a machine that appeared to be smoothly oiled and resistance-free, "Civil Disobedience" proposed an apparatus that slowly and steadily ground toward a halt without actually halting—a kind of Zeno's paradox of infinite deceleration, a government of the least governed.

Given the social rifts that shaped "Civil Disobedience," it's not surprising the essay was so popular in the 1960s, as I was coming of age. For the war against Mexico, substitute the Vietnam War; for Manifest Destiny, the Truman Doctrine and the "domino theory"; for the abolition movement, the civil rights movement; and for the policy of Indian removal, the American Indian Movement. The parallels were hard to miss, and Thoreau's aphoristic, rebellious exhortation to conscience and self-awareness suited a decade that also produced Dr. Martin Luther King Jr. and Abbie Hoffman. Not only that, but in the eyes of a rising generation of baby-boomers, "Civil Disobedience" pointed to something more than politics. Many saw it as a blueprint for a more liberated or engaged *identity*, even though it sometimes led to a rather trite and confused notion of "dropping out." The essay had the energy and certainty of youth, it accentuated individual conscience, and not even Holden Caulfield could call it phony. It also upheld a doctrine of *against* that was typical of everything from the lunch-counter sit-in to the so-called counterculture. Little wonder that when Thoreau changed his name from David Henry to Henry David, he just did it on his own instead of following the law that required him to petition the state legislature.

Still, for the majority of people today—and certainly for myself—Thoreau the lone wolf and political dissident has largely given way to Thoreau the environmental activist. Now that we face the uncertainties of global warming, while suffering more than ever from what the writer Richard Louv has termed "nature-deficit disorder," that's how he seems most relevant. In the essay "Walking," first delivered as a lecture in the years before *Walden* was published, Thoreau's opening words are, "I wish to speak a word for Nature, for absolute freedom and wildness, as contrasted with a freedom and culture merely civil." Because of that essay, and because of everything that came after it, Thoreau has become the most acclaimed voice in American environmentalism and natural history writing. The year 2017 marked the bicentennial of his birth, and like the path around Walden Pond, his words now form a continuous loop in the American imagination.

But I have often wondered: Do people see Thoreau as a man of the past or a modern man? Is he strictly a nostalgic figure, or does our pulse still beat with his the way his beat with nature? Have we ceased to struggle with his provocative ideas, or do we still think of them as animate and prickly?

If we go by the way Thoreau has been canonized, I would say it's the former. Not only are the sort of scholarly essays that make up a work like *Thoreauvian Modernities* few and far between, but many radical environmentalists prefer a simplistic slogan like "Back to the Pleistocene!" to the sort of hybrid, negotiated conservationism that Jonathan Franzen struggles with in his novel *Freedom*. More than a few self-described

Detroit Publishing Company, *Thoreau's Cove, Concord, Mass,* c. 1908.
Photograph from glass negative, 8 x 10 in. Courtesy of Library of Congress
Prints and Photographs Division, Washington, D.C.

environmentalists can stand spellbound before Ansel Adams's photographs of Yosemite Valley while pointedly turning their backs on Robert Adams's photographs of Colorado Springs and its suburbs—which are no less beautiful or alert to nature.

As it happens, my own interest in Thoreau has largely been refracted through a lens of modern science, art, and literature. I'm the son of a marine geologist who helped to prove the theory of plate tectonics, and for more than twenty years I was a conceptual artist. Over and over again I've found that what I've learned from Thoreau, and what I love or doubt

Dennis Oppenheim, *Directed Seeding*, part of *Directed Seeding/Cancelled Crop*, 1969. The route from Finsterwolde (location of wheat field) to Nieuwe Scans (location of storage silo) was reduced by a factor of 6X and plotted on a 154 x 267 meter field. The field was then seeded following this line. In September the field was harvested in the form of an X. The grain was isolated in its raw state, further processing was withheld.... In this case the material is planted and cultivated for the sole purpose of withholding it from a product-oriented system. © Dennis Oppenheim. Courtesy of Dennis Oppenheim Estate.

about him, can be traced to this background. He seems especially relevant to the American land art movement of the 1960s and '70s, as well as to the more recent experimentation with genetic-based art and poetry. Both hark back to issues Thoreau was the first to raise, and both help to bring some of his more radical or provocative ideas into sharper focus—not just aesthetically, but morally.

I believe the land artist Robert Smithson was right to say that most people "have a kind of picture book sentimental, very trite romanticism of what the balance of nature is." He was also right to remind us that "there is no going back to Paradise or 19th century landscape which is basically what the conservationist attitude is." When Smithson explicitly distanced himself from "wishy-washy transcendentalism," he was merely acknowledging the extent to which Thoreau in particular had become identified with a retrospective or imaginary version of wilderness. In fact, we're more prone than ever to associate both Walden Pond and Thoreau himself with some Eden-like state of nature—pristine woods, not cultivated woodlots.

But Smithson was wrong about Thoreau—just as the architect and cultural critic Rem Koolhaas was wrong to say, "We used to renew what was depleted, now we try to resurrect what is gone." In fact, Thoreau was among the earliest to see that Americans were already depleting the environment and that what was gone was gone—sometimes so far gone that it had receded into myth. At the same time, he was also among the earliest to argue that even the most peripheral or "wasted" aspects of the landscape could be as wild as the nature that was being lost. He spent most of his waking life examining the sort of life that thrived along the derelict edges of a tilled field or in the heart of a dense and muddy swamp.

Though Thoreau might be called a recovering romantic, I suspect Smithson would have felt differently if he'd known the Thoreau whose journal reads, "It is in vain to dream of a wildness distant from ourselves. There is none such. It is the bog in our brain and bowels, the primitive vigor of Nature in us, that inspires that dream. I shall never find in the wilds of Labrador any greater wildness than in some recess in Concord." Rather than pointing to some virgin land that may or may not have existed in the past, Thoreau preferred to focus on what he could find within a ten-mile radius of his home—something the philosopher Ludwig Wittgenstein later referred to as "arranging what we have always known." His daily walks were a kind of experiment in seeing. Moving to Walden Pond was an experiment in writing. And perceiving the beauty of an ordinary apple tree was "a moral test."

Thoreau's desire to elevate nature by featuring its most humble aspects is just one of many things that make me think of his work as modern, not dated or wishy-washy. Warhol, too, was a master of the everyday materials of life, and many other modern and postmodern artists and writers have taken this aesthetic to even greater lengths. To read *Walden* as Thoreau seems to have written it—not just wide awake but alert at all times to what he called "a different intention of the eye"—is to see why the modest, hybrid landscape of Concord was so important to him and why it ought to be important to us as well. Thoreau wasn't pushing us to see the world through his eyes, exactly as he saw it. Instead, he wanted us to see the sort of things we *might* see if we only looked for ourselves—including the interval he opened up between *Walden* and Walden.

In the end, Thoreau didn't *discover* the landscape of Concord and Walden Pond so much as *invent* it. And *by* inventing it, he became what Stanley Cavell has called the number one "watchman" of American nature, the singular cry in the wilderness that compelled his contemporaries to begin listening to what he had to say about nature. The first cut *was* the deepest when a description of the Deep Cut above Walden Pond—a machined notch softened by melting sands—made people see that "the earth is not a mere fragment of dead history, stratum upon stratum like the leaves of a book, to be studied by geologists and antiquaries chiefly, but living poetry like the leaves of a tree, which precede flowers and fruit,—not a fossil earth, but a living earth."

If we continue to heed Thoreau today, continue to seek the greater sympathy with nature he made so much of, it's mainly because his living poetry shows how crucial it is to understand the living earth, both for ourselves and for the sake of Earth itself. Of course, there's no getting past the sheer complexity of his work—not when a single page of his can veer from Aristotle, Confucius, and Darwinian evolution to the defects of William Wordsworth's poetry. But the more we learn *about* Thoreau, the more we learn *from* him. And that begins with a basic understanding of how the man christened David Henry Thoreau became the naturalist and writer Henry David Thoreau.

CHAPTER 1

Concord

Henry David Thoreau was born just outside the town of Concord, Massachusetts, on July 12th, 1817. Except for a brief period in Chelmsford and Boston as a young child, and an even briefer stay on Staten Island as a young man, he lived his entire life in or around Concord—eventually succumbing to tuberculosis on the morning of May 6th, 1862, mournfully prayed over by his mother, his sister, and a favorite aunt. Reduced to its basics, a short biography of Thoreau might read, "Lived a quiet life in a small town." But if such a biography were to be illustrated, one of Edward Hopper's scenes of introspective solitude would be a far better choice than one of Norman Rockwell's congenial slices of New England life. "Young men were born with knives in their brain," Ralph Waldo Emerson wrote years later, "a tendency to introversion, self-dissection, anatomizing of motives."

Historians have generally had a hard time picturing Thoreau's looks and demeanor. He was photographed only twice—both headshots, both taken late in life—and what you notice most is how fast his health was declining. The handful of drawings and busts we have of him swerve from caricature to romantic hagiography, and the same thing is true of the various diaries, journals, and newspaper reports that mention or describe him. At every turn, the picture that emerges depends on who's talking, including Thoreau himself.

Evidently, he was about five feet, seven inches tall, with a slim build, light brown hair, narrow, sloping shoulders, long arms, short legs, a receding forehead and chin, a large nose, deep-set blue-gray eyes, and a beard he began to grow late in life to protect against colds. His best friend, Ellery Channing, said that Thoreau's "features were quite marked:

the nose aquiline or very Roman, like one of the portraits of Caesar," his "eyes expressive of all shades of feeling," his forehead "full of concentrated energy and purpose." Nathaniel Hawthorne, who usually found Thoreau exasperating, thought he was "ugly as sin, long-nosed, queer-mouthed," but admitted "his ugliness is of an honest and agreeable fashion, and becomes him much better than beauty." By his own admission, Thoreau had trouble looking people in the face, and a Harvard classmate commented that his "eyes seldom left the ground, even in his most earnest conversation with you"—suggesting that he might be added to the growing list of those retrospectively diagnosed with some form of autism, including Immanuel Kant, Charles Darwin, and Ludwig Wittgenstein. Other contemporaries reported that Thoreau spoke in a "staccato style" and had a slight speech defect that made it difficult for him to pronounce the letter *r*; that he was a "great talker," but often conversed in the form of a monologue, sitting with his head bent over, staring at the floor; and that he was either an indifferent lecturer or had listeners rolling in the aisles. According to Sophia Hawthorne, he ice-skated with an impromptu, free-form display of "dithyrambic dances and Bacchic leaps," and yet he was also said to walk "Indian style"—apparently a variation of "Indian file"—which, as I understand it, called for the disciplined, unnatural act of putting one foot directly in front of the other. Emerson tells us, "His senses were acute, his frame well-knit and hardy, his hands strong and skilful in the use of tools. And there was a wonderful fitness of body and mind." Since Thoreau was ill off-and-on his entire life, it appears the rigorous energy and purpose others responded to was largely an extension of the single-minded resolve that was so much a part of his morality and intelligence. Like the Caesar of Lucan's *Pharsalia*, he felt disgraced by inactivity.

Thoreau's attachment to Concord was almost primal: as much instinct and memory as inclination or opportunity. A family story, recounted in Walter Harding's fine biography, has it that when Thoreau's mother told him after college that he should strap on a knapsack and seek his fortune elsewhere, tears suddenly welled in his eyes and he had to be soothed by his sister—who put her arm around him, kissed him, and said he could stay. That this was one of the few occasions Thoreau was known to cry shows how closely he identified his life with Concord.

Still, I can't help comparing him to Montaigne, for example, who led a long and active life, both in love and battle, before returning home to write his famous essays. Only in the seclusion of his library did Montaigne invoke his hero Socrates—a man more willing to die than be exiled—as he advised his readers not to go far away because they had plenty to do at home. Thoreau himself could only speak from imagination, not from the resistance and fatigue of experience, when he in turn echoed Montaigne, writing in his journal, "Cleave to the simplest ever. Home,—home,—home," and "I have a real genius for staying at home." Doubtless he was speaking more metaphorically than literally when he said that his life was "as adventurous as Crusoe's—as full of novelty as Marco Polo's, as dignified as the Sultan's, as momentous as that of the reigning prince." These words may sound especially hollow to anyone (and I include myself) who's actually been to Asia or put ashore on the South Pacific islands where Alexander Selkirk, the real-life model for Robinson Crusoe, was voluntarily marooned for four years.

On the other hand, we shouldn't forget that the urge to return home became so strong on Magellan's long voyages that he had to forbid any talk of turning back, while Vasco da Gama responded to the same urge by keeping a single set of maps and instruments for himself and dumping the rest overboard. During the Civil War, Union generals were so worried about deserters that they eventually banned the song "Home Sweet Home." Thoreau merely elevated this love of home—this all-out "reverence for home," in the words of literary historian Peter Blakemore—to the level of a natural philosophy, a worldview.

Thoreau's reluctance to leave home has suffered the usual psychological probing. Some have said that he loved his domineering, charismatic mother, who was both a "born talker" and a "born reformer," far too much to leave. Others have said that he wanted to cultivate his image as a ne'er-do-well, a slacker, to cover for his father's low-energy management of the family's pencil factory; or that, on the contrary, he actually hoped to supplant his father by taking over the family business; or that, worst of all, he saw his brother John, both more easily liked and in love with the same woman, as such an unconscious rival that the guilt he felt when John died of tetanus wouldn't allow him to leave the scene of the psychic crime.

I generally find these explanations interesting but not very useful. Gustave Flaubert never married, lived most of his life with his dear mother, wouldn't allow his lovers even to meet her, and convinced his housekeeper to wear one of his mother's favorite dresses around the house for years after she died. Thoreau also remained unmarried, also lived with his mother, would usually relate to a woman as if she were a sister or "a catholic virgin mother," and was said to politely tolerate his mother's interruptions at the dinner table before resuming where he'd left off as if she'd never spoken. What does this really tell us about these writers, each of whom spent almost his entire life in or near his birthplace? What does it tell us about the *life* they lived there, or how that life shaped the essays and books that make them worth wondering about in the first place? I suppose Thoreau would have agreed with one of Flaubert's superb dicta: "Be regular and orderly in your life, so that you may be violent and original in your work." But were their respective birthplaces elemental or incidental, absolutely necessary to their work or mere background to a family dynamic that could have existed elsewhere?

Concord was a small town at heart. When a section less than a mile from the town center first opened up, it was popularly known as "Texas" because it seemed as distant as the territory about to be annexed by the United States. Not surprisingly, such insularity led to a number of petty squabbles and longstanding feuds. At least one of these was endemic, having gotten to the point where both the town as a whole, and Thoreau's own family, were split between those who went to one church and those who went to another. Most things, however, played out on a smaller scale. A good example is the time Thoreau came down the stairs to find Channing and his mother, who never liked each other, standing back-to-back on the front doorstep, both with arms folded, neither willing to say anything or give any ground. Another is the time he and a friend started a cooking fire that quickly blew out of control—burning something over a hundred acres of land, causing two thousand dollars in damages, and provoking such anger that several townspeople called Thoreau a "woods-burner" till the day he died. These same haters were part of a much larger group put off by the way Thoreau supposedly refused to work more than six weeks a year and chose to hole up at Walden Pond for as long as he liked.

Of course, Thoreau was criticized most often for appearing to *flaunt* his "negative superiorities," as Robert Louis Stevenson called them in a mostly friendly testimonial. While still a boy, Thoreau was known as "the Judge," and some of his classmates took to calling him "the fine young scholar with the big nose"—referring, I suppose, not only to its size, but to his apparent habit of looking down it. Hawthorne would later claim that "in his presence one feels ashamed of having any money, or a house to live in, or so much as two coats to wear, or of having written a book that the public will read," and the editor George William Curtis would add that "it was like the reproof of the statue of a god."

Even those who admired Thoreau often found him dry and aloof: the sort of person who, in Heinrich Böll's choice phrase, was more likely to offer you a glass of H_2O than water. Plainly, there were times when Thoreau seemed to view the people of Concord not as a community of neighbors, but as an audience or congregation needing to be reprimanded or edified. No matter what, he was clearly more comfortable speaking to many of them from behind a lectern than over a picket fence. The lasting exceptions were some outlying farmers, with whom he regularly discussed natural history, and the town children, who seemed to soften his standoffishness as soon as they approached and were usually welcomed with open arms.

"He was a born protestant," Emerson declared in a celebrated eulogy of Thoreau that was neither hagiographic nor entirely accurate. Emerson went on to say that "few lives contain so many renunciations. He was bred to no profession; he never married; he lived alone; he never went to church; he never voted; he refused to pay a tax to the State; he ate no flesh, he drank no wine, he never knew the use of tobacco; and, though a naturalist, he used neither trap nor gun." Indeed, it was almost "as if he did not feel himself except in opposition."

Another way of putting this is that Thoreau was a born moralist. As Emerson also said, he always wanted "a fallacy to expose, a blunder to pillory." I'm sure this occasionally came across as a resistant strain of narcissism—as if the only thing Thoreau saw reflected in the surface of Walden Pond was his own face. Walt Whitman intimated as much when he suggested that Thoreau "couldn't put his life into any other life—realize why one man was so and another man was not so"—a point echoed by Stevenson when he said that Thoreau was too devoid of weaknesses to "be truly polar with humanity." The editor and writer James Russell Lowell was even harsher: "Those who have most loudly advertised their passion for seclusion and their intimacy with nature, from Petrarch down, have been mostly sentimentalists, unreal men, misanthropes on the spindle side, solacing an uneasy suspicion of themselves by professing contempt for their kind." Is it any surprise that Thoreau was so often seen as a prig?

But human ethics have always relied on proximity, on a notion of *immediate* effect that excludes anyone from being condemned for murder, for example, who can't be placed at the scene of the crime or considered directly responsible for it. By setting himself so directly against the sort of values and beliefs that made Concord representative of the country as a whole, Thoreau developed an intensely visceral form of morality that was anchored by his life in Concord to the very values he sought to subvert and the very people and institutions he sought to criticize. Rather than being an abstract set of principles, blindly accepted, his was the sort of morality that grabbed people by the throat and forced them to think and feel. A perfect example is the night he was jailed for refusing to pay a poll tax that supported both slavery and a war against Mexico. Word of his jailing—which was voluntary, by the way, a deliberate act of resistance—quickly spread in Concord, and he later delivered a lecture at the Concord Lyceum that became the essay "Civil Disobedience."

Naturally, this oppositional temperament made him the conscience of Concord. What more could a Puritan town like Concord ask for than Thoreau's pitiless, outraged, austere—if often witty—sense of morality and justice? Not that Thoreau ever treated his moral opposition as anything other than moral suasion. If he was sometimes seen as a prig, it was never because he viewed himself as the second coming of Cotton Mather. The Concord lockup and lyceum were Thoreau's pulpit, not the knocked-together scaffolding of a Salem witch trial. We should never forget another of Emerson's eulogistic comments: "In any circumstance, it interested all bystanders to know what part Henry would take and what he would say."

Some critics have noted a defensive side to Thoreau's love of Concord that makes it seem his rebelliousness was mainly a mask, a need to overcompensate, because he lacked the courage to leave. Certainly, there could be a brittle, almost boastful quality to the way he endlessly sided with staying put. No one's likely to say of Thoreau what Lady Caroline Lamb said of the truly romantic traveler Lord Byron, that he was "mad, bad, and dangerous to know." On the other hand, I don't think Thoreau can be accused of fear or cowardice for remaining true to his birthplace. If anything, he faced the earliest test of his adult life with admirable aplomb.

The Panic of 1837, a financial meltdown marking the start of a recession that would last seven years, coincided with Thoreau's graduation from Harvard. His mother was not simply teasing, playing a cheap trick, when she told him to pack a bag and skedaddle. Despite an unusually mixed economy, Concord had become a commercial dead zone. Even farmers able to subsist found themselves unable to make much of a living. It wasn't long before many of the young men from town chose to join the thousands of other Americans moving westward—most of them, I might add, preserving a poignant, stubborn sense of home by adhering to the latitude they were born in. The lumber industry of the Northwest was built by settlers from Maine and New Hampshire, the cotton industry in Texas by tenant farmers from the Deep South.

Though Thoreau wasn't immune to this reality and sought teaching jobs as far away as Kentucky, he seemed to be going through the motions more than anything else, waiting patiently for his inertia to pay off. Soon he started a private school with his brother, and in the years that followed he worked for Emerson off and on, took over the family business, and became an expert surveyor—all of which created the economic elbow room for him to remain in Concord. Near the end of his life he would confide to his journal, "I have never got over my surprise that I should have been born into the most estimable place in all the world, and in the very nick of time, too." Since Thoreau was never asleep at the wheel of history, it's clear that he preferred to steer in a different direction from his fellow Americans—making his love of Concord a form of civil disobedience, not an act of cowardice or timidity. Nor did this direction ever waver. A journal entry from 1858, two years later, reads, "Take the shortest way round and stay at home."

Robert Frost once wrote that "the land was ours before we were the land's." But Concord was Emerson's home before it was Thoreau's—not chronologically, because Emerson actually moved there more than a decade after the Thoreau family had made it their home, but because he had become the leading light of literary New England. As soon as Thoreau felt the great man's radiance shine on him, he bent toward it like a phototropic plant. Indeed, Thoreau became so close to the illustrious writer that he was sometimes accused of wanting to *be* Emerson. Recalling the sycophants who used to bump into each other whenever the tyrant Dionysius the Elder was around—deliberately knocking things over to suggest they were as nearsighted as he was—several of Thoreau's critics declared that when they closed their eyes they couldn't tell whether Emerson or Thoreau was speaking. Apparently, it became a standing joke in certain circles, provoking the sort of smirking comments we might expect of high school students.

Virginia Woolf was much closer to the truth, I think, when she claimed in a hundredth-anniversary tribute to Thoreau that "the strongest natures, when they are influenced, submit the most unreservedly." One of the reasons Thoreau weathered the Panic of 1837 so confidently was that Emerson prompted him to start his journal that year, flattering him with the idea that he could be a writer. Emerson also introduced Thoreau to a circle of writers that included Margaret Fuller, Bronson Alcott, Elizabeth Peabody, and Theodore Parker. And from their first meeting, Emerson encouraged his disciple to explore the imperatives of a more elevated, more transcendental life—a life Thoreau may have already glimpsed as a boy when he told his mother, "I have been looking through the stars to see if I could see God behind them." A very early journal entry reads, "My desire is to know *what* I have lived, that I may know *how* to live henceforth." What he later wrote in *Walden* was merely the seed rising up as the tree: "Every man is tasked to make his life, even in its details, worthy of the contemplation of his most elevated and critical hour." No wonder 1837 was also the year he changed his name from David Henry to Henry David, already sensing that he had to *make* a name for himself, had to *create* his genius, by aligning himself more singularly with the world.

"Genius" doesn't mean the same thing now as it did in Thoreau's day. For us, it's mainly a mark of intelligence—though not just of a high IQ, but of a type of intelligence or talent that seems mysterious and inspired, perhaps a gift of the gods. If I've gotten the story right (it came to me secondhand), I'd cite the time Murray Gell-Mann, the physicist who first described the quark, attended a lecture at Caltech that included about a hundred slides. Like several others during the discussion period afterward, Gell-Mann raised his hand to ask a question. But the question was unusual enough to catch everyone by surprise, and he was able to illustrate it by referring to a particular slide in the sequence—having counted them automatically as they were projected.

As wonderful as this feat may be, it's not something that Thoreau and his contemporaries would have responded to with an admiring, "Pure genius." For them, genius was a matter of finding out who we are ideally meant to be. Aristotle had argued that every being is defined by a nature that is a principle, a cause, and a substance all rolled into one, while the ancient Greeks and Romans viewed genius—literally, innate ability, inborn nature—as the guiding spirit of a fate we are either born with no memory of or know only partially until we wake up to it. The philosopher Plotinus, a favorite of both Emerson's and Thoreau's, claimed that genius also means "coming into this particular body and being born of these particular parents, and in such and such a place, and in general what we call the external circumstances." This belief paralleled the Romans' belief in *genius loci*—the protective spirit of a place—which later became important in British landscape theory as the more secular "genius of the place."

That Thoreau was trafficking in this classical view of genius is apparent in journal entry after journal entry from the late 1830s to the early 1850s. He alludes to it when he says that "every man is a warrior when he aspires" and "the noble life is continuous and unremitting," and it's what he means when he says, "my genius dates from an older era than the agricultural." In 1841 he complained, "I don't want to feel as if my life were a sojourn any longer. That philosophy cannot be true which so paints it. It is time now that I begin to live." Imagine how he felt a decade later, having gloomily concluded, "Here I am 34 years old, and yet my life is almost wholly unexpanded. How much is in the germ! There is such an interval between my ideal and the actual in many instances that I may say I am unborn." Though I wouldn't call this long, strange period of uncertainty an extended adolescence, as several biographers have, Thoreau undoubtedly felt tortured for many years by his apparent inability to remember or wake up to his genius.

Thoreau's writings are filled with references to the state of being asleep or awake, as when he says in *Walden*, "Little is to be expected of that day, if it can be called a day, to which we are not awakened by our Genius, but by the mechanical nudgings of some servitor." The implications of this reference are probably lost on modern readers—not least of all because it also evokes the Second Great Awakening, a series of religious revivals that swept the country during the early 1800s. Of course, romanticism made a myth of authenticity and genius—the more extreme, the better—and modernism turned originality into its raison d'être. But today these concepts exist as little more than fallen, or jaded, or essentially self-reflexive notions. Why do we so readily use the word "authentic" to describe a politician who's willing to express an ignorant or idiotic opinion just because it's deeply felt? And what do we mean when we speak of the originality of Andy Warhol's work or the body of work known as "uncreative writing"? "I don't think that there's a stable or essential 'me,'" the poet and essayist Kenneth Goldsmith has explained. "That can mean adopting voices that aren't 'mine,' subjectivities that aren't 'mine,' political positions that aren't 'mine,' opinions that aren't 'mine,' words that aren't 'mine' because, in the end, I don't think that I can possibly define what's mine and what isn't." When Warhol sent someone to masquerade as him on *The Tonight Show*, he effectively erased the difference between modern and postmodern versions of genius. Certainly, it's fitting, if merely coincidental, that one of his first and most "original" films showed nothing more than a man sleeping for five hours and twenty minutes. Acknowledging the paradoxical status of such work, critic Marjorie Perloff has recently proposed the concept of "unoriginal genius."

None of this would have made sense to Thoreau. From the moment he began his iconic journal he wanted to feel the urgency, the burden of *necessity*, epitomized by the theologian who Jorge Luis Borges refers to in one of his gnomic stories—a man who believes that no one should even taste a glass of water without justification. Channing once claimed that "no matter where he might have lived, or in what circumstances," Thoreau "would have been a writer." But Channing was only half right. It's true the early pages of the journal are filled with brief quotes from Goethe, Carlyle, and de Quincey, as well as the first drafts of various essays and lectures, and we can see the searing need to put things into words, the playful fascination with language itself. Thoreau plainly thought of himself as a writer. What he seemed to lack was a compelling

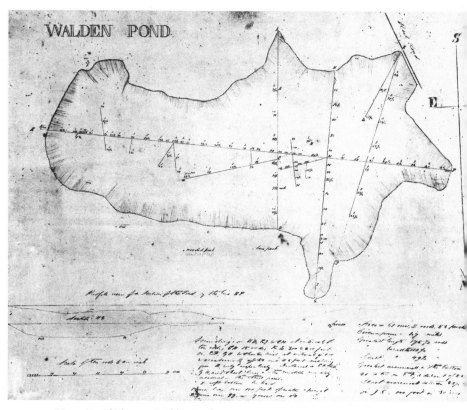

Henry David Thoreau, *Walden Pond*, manuscript survey, [1846].
Ink on paper. Courtesy of Concord Free Public Library.

sense of authenticity or legitimacy—as if what he was writing *about* was
somehow arbitrary, not basic; expedient, not imperative; derivative, not
original; stillborn, not alive—because he had not fully awakened to his
genius. After all, the journal was supposed to be about *him*. But who was
he? Apparently being a born protestant wasn't enough. Neither was being a born writer. Surely he would have shunned Roland Barthes' claim
that a text written by a scoundrel and a text written by a saint could both
rise to the level of great literature.

Fortunately, Concord itself became Thoreau's wake-up call, proving
that his genius derived from a particular time and place. And Emerson,
as so often happened in the early years of Thoreau's career, played the

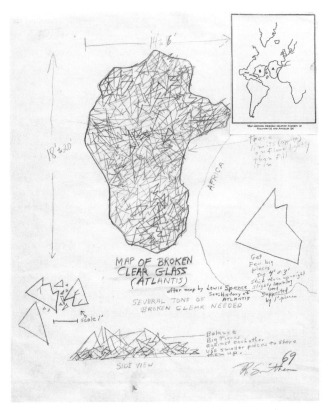

Robert Smithson, *Map of Broken Clear Glass (Atlantis)*, 1969. Collage, photostat, map, graphite on paper, 16¾ x 14 in. Courtesy of James Cohan, New York. Art © Holt-Smithson Foundation/Licensed by VAGA, New York, N.Y.

role of alarm clock. As did the year 1837. Indeed, Emerson's enduring influence on Thoreau might be reduced to a single phrase from that year: "The ancient precept, 'Know thyself,' and the <u>modern precept, 'Study nature,' become at last one maxim.</u>"

One of the most notable features of nineteenth-century art and literature was the way it magnified the struggle of consciousness to know itself. But nothing was more vital to transcendentalists like Emerson and Thoreau than a consciousness of nature. Remarkable as it may seem now, such insights did not come easily to Thoreau. Only slowly, hesitantly— lurching from one approach to another—was he able to identify with the nature around him. A year after wondering when he would begin to live his life, he took a literal approach, noting in the journal, "I feel that I draw nearest to understanding the great secret of my life in my closest intercourse with nature." That same year he waxed more metaphorical: "I will wait the breezes patiently, and grow as Nature shall determine. My fate cannot but be grand so." A few years later, indicating that he'd awakened early to bathe in Walden Pond, he turned to metaphor again: "The morning must remind everyone of his ideal life— Then if ever we can realize the life of the Greeks. We see then Aurora. The morning brings back the heroic ages."

These were merely tantalizing hints, however. Only as Thoreau became alert to the heroic age of childhood would he truly discover his ideal life. Here, too, there was an auroral link to the classical world he found so noble and inspiring, in that the first stage of Thoreau's personal education began with the literature, mythology, and history commonly identified with the cradle of civilization. But this cultural version of ontogeny recapitulating phylogeny was only part of what Thoreau was after, and the least important part at that. For it was Thoreau's *memories* of childhood that revealed the genius he believed he was born with, but had yet to remember or wake up to.

———

Thoreau's easygoing relationship with children was symptomatic of a mind that continually harked back to its youth. Channing was again half right when he said that Thoreau "was one of those who keep so much of the boy in them that he could never pass a berry without picking it." While true, Thoreau's apparently nostalgic attitude was thornier, more philosophical than that, and very specific to his birthplace. A journal entry from 1851, when the journal as a whole was morphing from a collection of miscellaneous comments and practice essays into a detailed record of the local landscape and climate, shows a writer trying to come to terms with a childhood spent mostly out of doors in the countryside around Concord.

"In youth before I lost any of my senses," Thoreau reminisced, "I can remember that I was all alive and inhabited my body with inexpressible satisfaction; both its weariness and its refreshment were sweet to me." Obviously, most of us feel this loss as we get older. Age is often experienced most painfully as a withering or failure of the body, at least in part because the section of the brain which enhances the intensity of our senses reaches a peak during our teenage years before gradually tapering off. In addition, there's always the romantic urge to *feel* something before we *think* it, which probably derives from the sensory lushness of childhood and adolescence as well. But Thoreau was in his mid-thirties at the time, neither adolescent nor old, and he was making a larger point about his place in the world—a world he seems to relate to retrospectively: "I think that no experience which I have to-day comes up to, or is comparable with, the experiences of my boyhood. And not only is this true, but as far back as I can remember I have unconsciously referred to the experience of a previous state of experience."

Though it isn't clear from this wistful and analytical passage, Thoreau usually had one particular childhood experience in mind. Another journal entry, written just after moving to Walden Pond, is worth quoting at length:

> Twenty-three years since, when I was five years old, I was brought from Boston to this pond, away in the country,—which was then but another name for the extended world for me,—one of the most ancient scenes stamped on the tablet of my memory, the oriental Asiatic valley of my world, whence so many races and inventions have gone forth in recent times. That woodland vision for a long time made the drapery of my dreams. That sweet solitude my spirit seemed so early to require that I might have room to entertain my thronging guests, and that speaking silence that my ears might distinguish the significant sounds. Somehow or other it at once gave the preference to this recess among the pines, where almost sunshine and shadow were the only inhabitants that varied the scene, over that tumultuous and varied city, as if it had found its proper nursery.

In the end, Thoreau didn't become "Thoreau" until he figured out that the most basic elements of his worldview—what Rainer Maria Rilke would call his "world-inner-space"—could be traced to his childhood memories of the landscape surrounding Walden Pond. I'd say he actually had a precocious feeling for nature, since studies have shown that most children that age are fearful of nature or behave in a domineering way toward it, while he instinctively felt the sort of bond we now refer to as biophilia. But his was the intimacy and love of a singular place and time. If Emerson seemed to identify with a rather abstract view of nature—something he vaguely termed "an original relation to the universe"—Thoreau woke up to the far more direct and verdant memory of a "proper nursery." That memory was the "*point d'appui,*" the "hard bottom and rocks in place," he made so much of in *Walden*. It was the durable state of mind he identified with morning, with rising "early and fast"; it was the basaltic, impervious reality he sought beneath the "alluvion" of opinion, prejudice, and tradition; it was the prototype for what he came to call a "life in nature." No wonder he kept returning to the pond day after day, both literally and as a concept.

Of course, Thoreau's broader name for the extended world of the pond was Concord. "I think I could write a poem to be called 'Concord,'" he muses in a journal entry from 1841, subtly superimposing the natural history of the pond onto the nearby village. "For argument I should have the River, the Woods, the Ponds, the Hills, the Fields, the Swamps and Meadows, the Streets and Buildings, and the Villagers. Then Morning, Noon and Evening, Spring, Summer, Autumn and Winter, Night, Indian Summer, and the Mountains in the horizon." There's something almost naïve about this imagined poem, as if it were a picture drawn by a child or a version of the house-tree-person test now used by clinical psychologists and art therapists. And, like his magnificent journal, which eventually amounted to nearly two million words, the poem appears to be both whole and unfinished at the same time. Samuel Beckett once suggested that a work of art could be a "total object, complete with missing parts, instead of partial object. Question of degree." The same thing could be said of Thoreau's "Concord."

Even before he wrote the poem, Thoreau decided to limit his *emotional* horizon to a "circle of ten miles' radius" around Concord, creating a sphere that encompassed Walden Pond and became both the boundary of his daily walks and the *ultima Thule* of his relatively short life span. Concord signified a kind of magic circle for Thoreau: a microcosm of recollection, a wheel of perpetually remembered possibility, a metaphorical container for everything he later had to say about nature. Emily Dickinson would call this sensibility "carrying a circumference"; William Faulkner would call it Yoknapatawpha County. But just as the ancient Romans believed the walls of their city could contain the entire human race, so Thoreau believed his ten-mile radius could encompass the entire world. "Be native to the universe," he writes in the journal. "I, too, love Concord best, but am glad when I discover, in oceans and wildernesses far away, the materials out of which a million Concords can be made." What makes this so special is that Thoreau was not simply isolating himself, creating a purely private Concord, but thinking of

Concord as the rest of the world might see it. The great paradox of his emotional horizon was that by going inward he was going outward at the same time.

Concord was the origin, the starting point, of an ardent and original philosophical system that kept returning to that starting point: not to remain static, not to retain the old landscape, but to rediscover and re-invent a new landscape with each revolution of the sun and the seasons. Thoreau often spoke of seeing something commonplace in a new light or for the first time. He didn't perceive nature as if it were a landscape painting or a still life—*nature morte*. Instead he saw it as an animated, evolving, essentially open-ended system that had to be understood over time to be understood at all. How could he describe the symbiotic rela-tionship between domesticated oxen and wild apple trees unless he was able to observe the same meadow for years on end? How could he say that a reddening maple tree "deserved well of Mapledom" unless he had studied "a thousand little well-behaved Maples" as they grew to adult-hood and met autumn on their own terms? "How much, what infinite, leisure it requires, as of a lifetime, to appreciate a single phenomenon!" he mused in the journal. "You must camp down beside it as for life, hav-ing reached your land of promise, and give yourself wholly to it. It must stand for the whole world to you, symbolical of all things."

Ultimately, Concord emerged as Thoreau's spatial baseline for the "whole world"—and the memory of his first visit to Walden Pond as the temporal and somatic origin of that baseline. "Nature must be viewed humanly to be viewed at all," he insists; "that is, her scenes must be asso-ciated with humane affections, such as are associated with one's native place." Without the intimacy and stability of Concord he had nothing reliable to measure change against, including the changes in his own life and affections. Even his rebelliousness was largely a response to that constant environment. Emerson could not have been more wrong when he concluded that Thoreau's habit "of extolling his own town and neigh-borhood as the most favored centre for natural observation" was merely "a whim which grew on him by indulgence." Thoreau's genius was clearly a genius of place—and that place was Concord. When he finally awoke to the genius of Concord, he awoke to the genius of *home*.

CHAPTER 2

Walden

Henry David Thoreau's private experiment at Walden Pond is probably the most noteworthy event in the history of American environmentalism. Countless numbers of people have read his book about the experience and every year nearly half a million admirers find the time to see the quiet, unassuming pond for themselves. The memorial cairn that marks the site of Thoreau's cabin has existed since the 1870s.

On the whole, this two-year interval has been treated as an effort to "simplify, simplify," to live life closer to the bone or off the grid. As Thoreau says in the opening paragraph of *Walden*, "I lived alone, in the woods, a mile from any neighbor, in a house which I had built myself, on the shore of Walden Pond, in Concord, Massachusetts, and earned my living by the labor of my hands only." But the experiment seems more complex knowing this was also when Thoreau spent the night in jail recounted in "Civil Disobedience" and that he actually left the pond for several weeks to hike a remote region of Maine. All of these experiences helped to shape the account of Walden that we know as *Walden*.

This account is really what matters. For Thoreau's stay at Walden was the interval that finally allowed him to pinpoint his literary genius, gradually turning Concord into "the poem to be called Concord" and Walden into *Walden*. Though Ellery Channing was being a bit facetious when he referred to the rude cabin beside the pond as a "wooden inkstand," the description rings true. Thoreau went to Walden to find his voice and to put that voice on paper. He wasn't dropping out of society or the life of the nation but trying to locate his proper place in it. No one who made a point of moving to Walden on July Fourth was truly trying to drop out. Indeed, the very act of finding himself as a writer forced him to find an audience for his work. Even when he occasionally sounded like the exiled Rousseau, who claimed to need no audience because he despaired of ever reaching one again, he really had an ideal public in mind. Ludwig Wittgenstein was right to suggest that language is less about expressing our own state of mind than provoking a response in others.

If Thoreau emerged from his temporary seclusion as an unyielding "watchman" for nature, it was mainly because he imagined his public as sluggish, desperate, and alienated from the nature best suited to their identity as Americans. Of course, this public was such a perfect foil to his literary genius that Thoreau undoubtedly invented it more than discovered it. But then, no one had thought of the modern bureaucratic state as "Kafkaesque," either, until *The Trial* appeared. Certainly, many of the things Thoreau spoke about in *Walden* are more relevant today than when the book was published—as if we, who now see his writings as essential, are the audience he was fated to invent all along.

Writers have always had to find the mental space to work—a comfort zone, so to speak. Ernest Hemingway wrote standing up, in a pair of loose loafers, his feet firmly planted on the skin of an animal he'd shot. Gertrude Stein claimed that she wrote only an hour a day, but spent the other twenty-three hours figuring out what to say. Georges Simenon placed a number of sharpened pencils on his desk, discarded each one as its point became dull, and finished whatever he was working on when he reached the last pencil. William Thackeray had to be holding a pen in his hand before he got any ideas, and Samuel Johnson came up with his best ideas while riding in carriages. Friedrich Schiller wrote with his feet in ice water, Ivan Turgenev with his feet in hot water. René Descartes, Voltaire, and Marcel Proust all wrote in bed— though Proust's bed was sequestered in a cork-lined room. Hunter S. Thompson didn't feel right as a writer until he got his hands on an IBM Selectric typewriter.

That Thoreau chose to work at a plain desk or table, usually first thing in the morning, before he began the walk he'd mapped out for the day, seems pretty tame by comparison. Even when he moved to Walden his routine remained the same, as anyone who visits the displaced replica of his cabin can see. On the other hand, a more flamboyant or decadent set of habits would have violated his stoic approach to life. The ancient world was more than a model of genius to Thoreau; it was also his ideal of mental and bodily discipline. "The complete subjugation of the body to the mind," he notes in the journal, "prophesies the sovereignty of the latter over the whole of nature."

I wish that such comments—and there are many others like them in the journal—didn't suggest the doomed optimism of a man suffering from tuberculosis. They always strike me as being somewhat tragic. But at least they bring us back to Flaubert's example of being "regular and orderly in your life, so that you may be violent and original in your work." Almost everything Thoreau published reminds me more of the novelist William S. Burroughs than the naturalist John Burroughs—and not just him, but many of the cut-and-paste internet writers Kenneth Goldsmith discusses. Instead of working in a straightforward manner, advancing from beginning to end, Thoreau fashioned his oddly contradictory style by copying out various passages from the journal or other notes and then pasting them end to end. Many of the passages were written years apart and he often assembled them out of sequence or with no idea of sequence at all. "In the true natural order the order or system is not insisted on," Thoreau notes. "Each is first, and each last." Composition basically came down to juxtaposition.

Not that the journal itself was ever as raw or spontaneous as it sounded. Thoreau seemed to accept William Wordsworth's theory that poetry begins as "emotion recollected in tranquility." At one point he indicates that even his most detailed, impressionistic, or exciting accounts of nature were written retrospectively, not on the spot. "I succeed best," he explains, "when I *recur* to my experience not too late, but within a day or two; when there is some distance, but enough of freshness." Many of Thoreau's best descriptions—of which his account of the thawing railroad cut in *Walden* is probably the most transcendent—were based on observations made over several seasons or more. They're records of what *might* have happened in a single instance, but that *typically* happened if these phenomena were studied, tabulated, and given the proper emotional weight after the fact. Walt Whitman's notion of the "divine average" comes to mind.

Walden was an interval of space as well as time, and Thoreau's transitory retreat to the pond is a reminder that he was fascinated by the notion of intervals. Look almost anywhere in his work and you'll come across intervals of space and time. But there are also intervals of sight and sound, of poetry and science, of two different views of the same phenomenon. "What an immeasurable interval there is between the first tinge of moonlight which we detect, lighting with mysterious, silvery, poetic light the western slopes, like a paler grass, and the last wave of daylight on the eastern slopes!" he observes in the journal. "It is wonderful how our senses ever span so vast an interval, how from being aware of the one we become aware of the other." In the essay "Walking" he notes that "There are some intervals which border the strain of the wood-thrush, to which I would migrate,—wild lands where no settler has squatted it; to which, methinks, I am already acclimated." All of these references to intervals imply a double-edged state of in-betweenness. While Thoreau occasionally sought a "*point d'appui*"—"a hard bottom and rocks in place"—he seemed more comfortable among the slowly sliding sands of the Deep Cut or the still more treacherous waters of Gowing's Swamp. As much as he spoke of harmony and higher laws, he actually inhabited a world of edges, gaps, juxtapositions, interruptions, and displacements. In fact, he often derived his higher laws from very low ground. Describing a white water lily he happened to see one day (an incident that concludes the essay "Slavery in Massachusetts"), Thoreau joyously exclaims, "It bursts up so pure and fair to the eye, and so sweet to the scent, as if to show us what purity and sweetness reside in, and can be extracted from, the slime and muck of earth."

Of course, Thoreau's decision to live alone in the woods, a mile from his nearest neighbor, might be little more than the gesture of a romantic wannabe—and an empty or exaggerated gesture at that. Flaubert traveled to Egypt and Carthage, hung out with male and female prostitutes, and contracted the syphilis that plagued him for the rest of his life; Lord Byron swam the Bosporus, joined the revolutionaries in the Greek War of Independence, and died in Missolonghi at the age of thirty-six; Robert Louis Stevenson ended his equally brief and eventful life in Samoa. Romanticism was obsessed with the exotic or remote, and part of its legacy was the way it associated the lure of foreignness with the basic idea of aesthetics—suggesting that an artist or writer needed to seek an interval beyond the civilized world of Europe, or at least European cities, to create something new and meaningful in art or literature. Though Walden was only a comfortable mile southeast of Concord, Thoreau often acted like it was halfway round the world. A typical example is the journal entry in which he says that his life is "as adventurous as Crusoe's—as full of novelty as Marco Polo's, as dignified as the Sultan's." Since Thoreau was often called "the Robinson Crusoe of Walden Pond," many of his contemporaries seemed to accept this romantic scenario. But in the sphere of language and writing, Thoreau's stay at Walden was totally contrary to the foreign or exotic, especially the exotic. If anything, he was seeking the native simplicity and authenticity that would allow him to "Cleave to the simplest ever. Home,—home,—home."

Cynthia Ozick has written that Franz Kafka—born and raised in Prague, but one of the great German stylists—spent his entire life wondering whether he was entitled to the German language. Writing with her usual acumen and elegance, Ozick concludes that Kafka's greatest fear was not that the German language "did not belong to him, but that he did not belong to it." This insight leads her to say that Kafka "wrote German with the passion of an ingenious yet stealthy translator, always aware of the space, however minute, between his fear, or call it his idea of himself, and the deep ease of at-homeness that is every language's consolation."

Ozick's comments are a poignant reminder of what any writer faces when speaking a native language that's not indigenous but imported. What does it mean to feel "at home" in a nation that has long looked to a "mother country" for the meaning of home? How disorienting is it to discover that feeling "at home" may actually be a form of alienation rather than a natural or authentic sense of place? How damaging is it to know that you don't fully belong to your native language and that writing may be a subtle form of collaboration? Is it possible to subvert a linguistic space that gives you the power of speech in the first place? Does an authentic sense of place—a feeling of home—have to begin with a language of displacement? Maybe modernists, feeling the accumulated weight of history, wanted to follow Ezra Pound's precept and "Make it new!" But writers heavily burdened by the weight of a colonial or imported language have always had to "Make it mine!"

Since Thoreau was writing as an American, in English, and within the space of a former British colony, these were the sort of issues he had to deal with every day. There was a reason he began the essay "Walking" by declaring that he wished to "speak a word for nature." It hardly matters whether we interpret this to mean that nature was unable to speak for itself, not allowed to speak for itself, or speaking in a way that most people couldn't hear. The point was that even something as "natural" as American nature had been silenced by a language shaped by English landscape and culture. While still at Harvard, Thoreau had noted that American poets remained so besotted by John Keats and William Wordsworth that they were "prone to sing of skylarks and nightingales, perched on hedges, to the neglect of the homely robin-red-breast, and the straggling rail-fences of their own native land."

Sometimes Thoreau was tormented by this situation, sometimes he responded to it more amicably. But he could never ignore it. After all, it wasn't until 1846, or midway through his stay at Walden, that Britain and the United States finally signed the treaty that ended all British claims to territory below the forty-ninth parallel. Most Americans at the time were so unsure of their culture, or so indebted to British culture, that writers like Thoreau often found themselves ignored by their fellow citizens until their work was either published in Britain or reprinted in a British journal that then made its way back across the Atlantic. Willingly or not, the despotic Stamp Act had been replaced by the far more pernicious stamp of British approval.

Obviously, every writer seeks the right to speak. But Thoreau, like most nineteenth-century Americans, was almost forced to seek this right at home, among his everyday, Concord roots, rather than in the exotic locations favored by proto-modernists like Byron or true modernists like Flaubert. He would never be able to loosen the ties of colonialism by holding them dearer. He would never escape the space of colonialism by adding to its reach. In Emerson's words, he would simply be traveling "away from himself," carrying "ruins to ruins."

Instead of being a rather empty romantic gesture, then, Thoreau's storied experiment at Walden Pond was more like a self-induced interval of silence—a momentary refusal to speak—that eventually allowed him to speak in his own voice. He had alluded to this interval when he described Walden as "that sweet solitude my spirit seemed so early to require that I might have room to entertain my thronging guests, and that speaking silence that my ears might distinguish the significant sounds." By saying that Walden gave him the "room" he desperately needed, Thoreau implied that the solitude and silence he found there represented a kind of open space, a clearing, within the sphere of language, enabling him to transcend the linguistic boundaries of colonial culture.

In effect, Walden became the wooded clearing in which Thoreau had a chance to see the world with what he called "a different intention of the eye." "We cannot see anything," he wrote in words that would be familiar to any conceptual artist, "until we are possessed with the idea of it, take it into our heads,—and then we can hardly see anything else." Walden was the *somewhere else* that permitted Thoreau to possess the *something else*. It was the slightly displaced space that became his proper place—the "proper nursery" of both his authenticity and his authority as a writer. Consider how quickly Walden itself became a counter friction to the language and status of the American wilderness.

Before he moved to Walden, Thoreau knew almost nothing about the wilderness, and the little he did know was largely limited to books. Though he'd hiked to the top of Mount Greylock in Massachusetts and Mount Washington in New Hampshire, both were popular tourist destinations, equipped with viewing towers on top and places to stay nearby. His decision to briefly abandon the pond for a more remote peak in Maine was a different kind of departure for him. The interior of Maine was known for its dense and ample woods, not the sort of woodlots that dotted the region around Walden Pond. Aside from symbolizing what Europeans and Americans alike thought of as the most "American" form of landscape—even rougher than Thomas Cole's iconic scenes of the Catskills and Adirondacks—these woods plainly qualified as the sort of exotic, or at least distant, location favored by the romantics. Not only that, but Thoreau's desire to climb Mount Katahdin, Maine's highest mountain, was exactly the sort of sentiment that had inspired Wordsworth to visit the Swiss Alps as a young man and to end his immortal *Prelude* with an account of climbing Mount Snowdon in North Wales.

But as Thoreau zigzagged his way toward the isolated mountain, he quickly found the woods closing in around him, forcing him to shimmy up a tree every once in a while just to see where he was going. On the summit itself, the clouds were so thick and low that granite boulders morphed into ghastly figments of his imagination, and he never even reached the highest point. Meanwhile, over the course of the entire trip, he grew more and more frustrated with the unrelieved uniformity of the landscape. "What is most striking in the Maine wilderness," he complained, "is the continuousness of the forest, with fewer open intervals or glades than you had imagined" and everything "more grim and wild than you had anticipated." Today, we'd call this an isotropic space and note that a plenum can also be a void.

Once more, however, Thoreau found himself in an interval. On his way back down the mountain he stumbled into a rough, irregular clearing that seemed to be the result of a fire caused by either lightning or careless loggers. Since most of the plants were new and low to the ground, the area reminded him of a pasture grazed by moose and deer. But it also looked remarkably primitive and desolate, with jagged slivers of timber jutting into the clearing and dense, impenetrable patches of blueberries covering the ground. As he passed through the alarming zone, he suddenly realized that the wilderness he had looked forward to seeing was actually "something savage and awful": a girdling sphere of "forever untameable *Nature*" that was "vast and drear and inhuman."

This bleak epiphany occurred in the middle of Maine, in the middle of a trip that also occurred midway through his stay at Walden—one interval inside another interval inside another, like a nested series of Russian dolls—and it clearly unsettled Thoreau. "What is nature," he wondered, unless it includes "an eventful human life" and is associated with the sort of human affections that are also associated "with one's native place"? The wilderness Thoreau encountered in Maine seemed to exclude human affections altogether. It even resisted his effort to adequately *describe* it. Thoreau may have left Walden believing that wilderness would be a transient silence—yet another interval that would allow him to develop his own voice. But it turned out to be an absolute silence—a silence that excluded any possibility of speech or attachment, a clearing that collapsed in on itself like a black hole. Much of his earlier work had exhibited a kind of mannered inflation of language, as if he needed to make up for a world that fell short of his writing. In Maine the situation was reversed. There, he found that his writing fell dismally short of the world.

Thoreau's trip to Maine was so eye-opening that he eventually ruled out the wilderness as the prevailing image of his native place. On the one hand, he realized that he preferred to write from a space in between the wilderness and the city. On the other, he realized that this space would be a perfect foil to colonial culture, since Americans often tried to prove that the United States was superior to Britain by contrasting the smoggy slums of Manchester or London to the pristine woods of Maine or the Hudson Valley. Returning from a second trip to Maine years later, Thoreau remarked, "It was a relief to get back to our smooth, but still varied landscape. For a permanent residence, it seemed to me that there could be no comparison between this and the wilderness, necessary as the latter is for a resource and a background, the raw material of all our civilization. The wilderness is simple, almost to barrenness." Though this honest assessment can hardly be compared to Ronald Reagan's notorious comment, "If you've seen one redwood tree, you've seen them all," Thoreau made it plain that he wanted to put some distance between himself and the wilderness.

So it was that Walden emerged as the *home* Thoreau wanted his native language to inhabit, the place that was *dis*-placed just enough to be an authentic residence. There's a reason the first two chapters of *Walden* are a record of how he made the pond his home—from carting in the boards to build his one room cabin to planting the crops that were meant to keep him alive and be his livelihood at the same time. Indeed, the early chapters are filled with both caustic and commonsense observations about the "necessaries for life": food, shelter, clothing, and fuel. But the later chapters suggest a far more radical view of home, transforming Thoreau's stay at Walden into the truly original experiment hailed by John Burroughs and many others.

———————

One of the great pleasures of reading *Walden* is learning how Thoreau himself gradually learned to define home, not just as a house or building of some sort, but as a very singular and specific locality, explored in great depth, in sunlight and moonlight, season after season, over the course of a lifetime. At first, Walden looks like a sort of suburb or frontier: within hearing distance of the militia practicing on the Concord Common, yet far enough away to feel isolated. But by the end of the book it has become the small-scale *bioregion* Thoreau so presciently outlined in his plan for "the poem to be called 'Concord.'" Once he began to fully understand and inhabit this bioregion, Thoreau came to think of it as a "common dwelling" that included himself and all the plants and animals he shared it with. Because these plants and animals were so specific to Concord, his ongoing effort to live with them as neighbors was not a form of alienation but an authentic expression of place. And the same thing was true of his writing.

The key to Thoreau's stay at Walden was familiarity and permanence. This isn't to say Walden itself was permanent, or even familiar all the time. Reading one journal entry after another makes it clear that the same phenomenon could leave Thoreau standing stupefied with wonder one day, scratching his head the next, and completely indifferent the day after that. Nor could a bioregion really be defined as a bioregion without acknowledging the way it changed as well as the way it stayed the same. But Thoreau wanted to *name and measure* these changes— measure the changes themselves and measure his response to them— and that meant he had to be familiar enough with Walden, had to study it long enough, closely enough, to make an accurate survey. Walden was an interval of time as well as space. Home was a calendar as well as "the limits of an afternoon walk." Writing was a delay as well as a means to picture or point.

Let six journal entries stand in for the hundreds of other passages that might be used to show the network of associations—personal, scientific, domestic, natural, literary, national, transcendental—that bound Thoreau to Walden. Like many writers, he rode the same hobbyhorse year after year. But his journal is filled with so many scintillating descriptions, aphorisms, and one-liners that the critic Alfred Kazin was moved to say that it was unnatural for someone to write that well every day. So, think of the entries as typical, representative, rather than as "best-ofs."

> How much, what infinite, leisure it requires, as of a lifetime, to appreciate a single phenomenon! You must camp down beside it as for life, having reached your land of promise, and give yourself wholly to it.

I am interested in each contemporary plant in my vicinity, and have attained to a certain acquaintance with the larger ones. They are cohabitants with me of this part of the planet, and they bear familiar names. Yet how essentially wild they are!

I can hardly believe that there is so great a difference between one year and another as my journal shows. The 11th of this month last year, the river was as high as it commonly is in the spring, over the causeway on the Corner road. It is now quite low. Last year, October 9th, the huckleberries were fresh and abundant on Conantum. They are now already dried up.

Why should I hear the chattering of blackbirds, why smell the skunk each year? I would fain explore the mysterious relation between myself and these things. I would at least know what these things unavoidably are, make a chart of our life, know how its shores trend, that butterflies reappear and when, know why just this circle of creatures completes the world. Can I not by expectation affect the revolutions of nature, make a day to bring forth something new?

Here I have been these forty years learning the language of these fields that I may the better express myself. If I should travel to the prairies, I should much less understand them, and my past life would serve me but ill to describe them. Many a weed here stands for more of life to me than the big trees of California would if I should go there.

Why, the roots of letters are *things*. Natural objects and phenomena are the original symbols or types which express our thoughts and feelings, and yet American scholars, having little or no root in the soil, commonly strive with all their might to confine themselves to the imported symbols alone.

Thoreau went to Walden to write. But he went there to write as an *American*, for *other* Americans. Though he claimed that moving to the cabin on July Fourth was nothing more than an accident or coincidence, he wasn't being serious. He openly admitted that the cabin wasn't ready for winter, lacking caulked walls and a chimney to keep him warm. Yet it was finished enough to shield him from the summer rains and airy enough to welcome the summer breezes. He could have moved in anywhere from a month or so before that date to several months after it. To say that moving in on Independence Day was accidental was so patently untrue that it proved the opposite. Without doubt, he was there to brag as lustily as a raucous Concord rooster, not add his voice to all the Americans mimicking the melodious trilling of Keats's nightingale.

Thoreau chose to be a natural history writer because he believed it was the best way to express himself as an American. The opening paragraph of the Declaration of Independence invoked "the Laws of Nature and of Nature's God," and Jefferson's *Notes on the State of Virginia*, published in 1785 and still popular in Thoreau's day, contended that American nature was superior to European nature in every way. William Bartram's 1791 classic, *Travels through North and South Carolina*, made more or less the same case in much greater detail and was almost as widely read as Jefferson's *Notes*. Thoreau owned a copy of Bartram's *Travels*, quoted it on occasion, and seems to have been inspired by some of its more ecstatic passages.

Yet among the most widely read naturalist works of Thoreau's day were the reports that came out of the U.S. Army expeditions to the west and the many state-sponsored geological surveys being conducted at the time. The majority of these reports were written by trained naturalists, published as large editions by state and federal agencies, reprinted in pirated editions by commercial publishers, and excerpted in newspapers and journals across the country. Since Thoreau consumed these reports by the dozens, paying special attention to the surveys of Maine and Massachusetts, it's easy to see why he equated the life of a naturalist— and a natural history writer—with that of a true American.

Still, it was one thing to identify himself with the field of natural history and quite another to say that one ought to *live a life in nature*. As Thoreau put it in *A Week on the Concord and Merrimack Rivers*, the work he went to Walden to complete, "Men nowhere, east or west, live yet a *natural* life, round which the vine clings, and which the elm willingly shadows." Pointing in this direction implied that nature should be seen as something that existed for its own sake, not simply for the sake of human cultivation and use. Thus, he goes on to say that "man would desecrate it by his touch." Naturally, this put him at odds with all the neighboring farmers who felt that God had actually *created* the world to be cultivated and used, a belief that would also prompt Flaubert to say that most of the farmers he knew fancied the sun was just there to make the cabbages grow. But Thoreau was basically trying to reinvent the meaning of nature by reinventing the nature of home.

We often seek to discover, define, or renew ourselves by returning to a fresh or imaginary origin. That Thoreau's childhood memory of Walden became his point of origin—the moment and the place that marked the beginning of a universe that steadily expanded to the radius of an afternoon's walk—goes a long way toward explaining why he was such a contrary and combative figure in his own day and is still so relevant today. By identifying the very idea of home with a bioregion, not an artificial structure, Thoreau developed a sense of place that both began with nature and always came back to nature as a basic standard of life. Nature "is a fixed point whereby we may measure our departure," Emerson

Alfred Winslow Hosmer, *Walden Pond and cairn*, [1890s].
Courtesy of Concord Free Public Library.

remarks. "As we degenerate, the contrast between us and our house is more evident." Is it any wonder that virtually everything Thoreau wrote about nature looked back to Walden? His apparent departure to Walden was really a return that allowed him to reclaim it over and over again as the interval of his literary genius. Like Darwin's notion of evolution, his originality was a kind of revolutionary recurrence.

Surveyed on foot and written by hand, Thoreau's natural history of Walden broke new ground—ground we're still exploring today. Counterintuitively, perhaps, he envisioned Walden not as a place over-burdened by language, but as a kind of margin or frontier of the sayable. He began to examine this linguistic margin by adopting the Linnaean taxonomy of genus and species. "With the knowledge of the name," he writes in the journal, "comes a distincter recognition and knowledge of the thing." Naming things allowed Thoreau to distinguish between

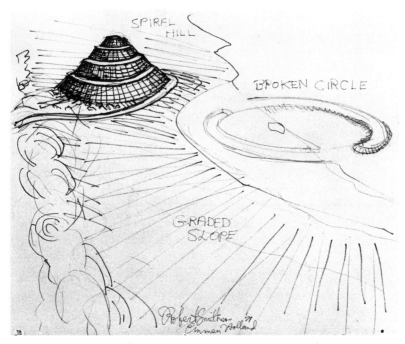

Robert Smithson, *Spiral Hill and Broken Circle*, 1971. Ink and pencil on paper, 12½ x 15½ in. Courtesy of James Cohan, New York. Art © Holt-Smithson Foundation/Licensed by VAGA, New York, N.Y.

Walden's indigenous plants and animals and the ones that had accidentally hitched a ride across the Atlantic or been deliberately imported to recreate the British landscape in America. In effect, the abstract and universal language of science made Walden a more specific and native place. But it also made Walden a more poetic and transcendental place. Gertrude Stein once said, "From the beginning until now and always in the future poetry will concern itself with the names of things." But Jorge Luis Borges made a more singular point: "There is no proposition that does not imply the entire universe; to say *the tiger* is to say the tigers that begot it, the deer and turtles devoured by it, the grass on which the deer fed, the earth that was mother to the grass, the heaven that gave birth to the earth."

Much of this semantic space could only be pointed to at the time, not pictured, or not adequately pictured. Botany made Thoreau's writing specific to Walden. Walden made it specific to the United States. And Thoreau's personal experience at Walden led him to believe the United States should pursue a more natural life. But he had to *invent a language* that combined all these concerns, creating the outlines of what we now think of as the language of American environmentalism. Both for him and for us it's a language that typically inhabits the interval between poetry and science—the interval between Gary Snyder and Edward O. Wilson, Annie Dillard and James Hansen—while also indicating the gap that separates what *can't* be said from what can. Bronson Alcott acknowledged this gap when he said that Thoreau was a seeker "of the Unseen through images of the Invisible."

I keep coming back to Thoreau's childhood memories of Walden as the origin of all that is most original about his work. Our strongest attachments to nature are often childhood attachments, and thus associated with an early sense of home. I've lived in New York City for over forty years, yet I still respond most viscerally to the landscape and climate of Southern California. The flowers that bloom in my head are the bougainvillea and hibiscus, not the daffodil and tulip; the trees that move me most deeply are the fog-shrouded eucalyptuses and scrub oaks, not the locusts, maples, and plane trees that shade the city's sidewalks. The writer Joseph Mitchell, an even longer-term immigrant in New York, felt so attached to his North Carolina childhood that he kept up a subscription to the local newspaper and used its weather section to estimate the depth of the county's streams from week to week. Obviously, Thoreau felt the same sense of attachment, but so strongly that he could never, ever move away from the Concord region.

Despite his sophisticated knowledge of nature and his stylish use of language, Thoreau always had the instincts of a child. Like Alice in Wonderland, he woke up each morning asking himself, "I wonder if I've been changed in the night? Let me think: was I the same when I got up this morning? I almost think I can remember feeling a little different. But if I'm not the same, the next question is: Who in the world am I?" To read Thoreau's work is not only to renew our own childhood memories of nature but our sense of childhood itself. There's something both comforting and intellectually rewarding about this. It keeps us on our toes by reminding us that we once ran barefoot. Certainly, it's hard to imagine a better way to approach *writing about* nature.

The only problem was that Thoreau's childhood coincided with a very insecure and *imported* sense of home. In order to *make* a home for himself he had to localize the English language and landscape, subverting the semantic space that gave him the power to speak in the first place. He was able to do this, was able to open up an interval within this space, by filling its outer margins. Susan Sontag famously related André Breton's notion of a "full margin" to an aesthetic of deviousness or voluntary impoverishment. Both Thoreau's move to Walden and his call to "simplify, simplify" align with her interpretation. But these intervals were not a prototype for something like Marcel Duchamp's *Anemic Cinema* or Andy Warhol's claim of making "nothing happen." Walden was more than just a denial or a negative. It was a *double negative* that proved positive. Very early in the journal, Thoreau notes that "double a deformity is a beauty." He would spend the rest of his life trying to negate the most alien or derogatory or misleading perceptions of American nature by accentuating its most negative and in-between aspects: the ragged, unmown edges of meadows; the dense, oozing swaths of swamps; the weed-infested strips next to walls; the gently thawing sands of the Deep Cut. These were the sorts of places that would only interest someone interested in nature to begin with.

What makes Thoreau so special, then, is that by making a home for himself he also helped to make natural history and environmentalism a crucial element of our American language and culture. Every view of nature is a creation story of some sort, whether it's the biblical Eden or the Big Bang theory, and over the course of time the picture of nature that Thoreau painted in *Walden* has become more and more important to the way we think of ourselves as both Americans and creatures of planet Earth. Thoreau's childhood has become ours, his view of home has become ours, his sense of nature has became ours—and it's apparent that we keep returning to *Walden* for much the same reasons he kept returning to Walden. To slightly amend Novalis, environmentalism "is properly homesickness; the wish to be everywhere at home."

CHAPTER 3

Walking

One of the better-known problems in mathematical theory arose several centuries ago when the people of Königsberg, which was then the capital of East Prussia, began to think about the route they took while wandering around the city's streets. Though now part of Russia and known as Kaliningrad, the city is still bisected by a river that once included two small islands connected to each other and to the banks on either side by seven bridges. The question was: could someone start and finish a walk in the same spot, without crossing any of the bridges more than once? In 1836 the Swiss mathematician Leonard Euler determined once and for all that the answer was no. His solution resulted in a diagram, referred to in modern terms as an Euler circuit, which inaugurated both graph theory and the idea of networks. Thus the simple act of walking transformed the everyday topography of Königsberg into the abstract field of topology—the science of connection.

Thoreau's own contribution to the science of connection began with an essay that translated the simple act of walking into the more elevated act of "sauntering." In the opening paragraphs of the essay "Walking," Thoreau suggests that sauntering is an old and honored word, "beautifully derived 'from idle people who roved about the country, in the Middle Ages, and asked charity, under pretense of going *à la Sainte Terre*,' to the Holy Land, till the children exclaimed, 'There goes a *Sainte-Terrer*,' a Saunterer." This fanciful etymology is so sly and double-edged that Thoreau may have been trying to transform the self-lacerating pilgrimages of the Middle Ages into the height of idleness and duplicity. But he goes on to associate sauntering with the "knights of a new, or rather an old, order"—"not the Knight, but Walker Errant"—while insisting that "you must be born into the family of the Walkers." Naturally, the walkers he had in mind, the ones who truly understood "the art of Walking," had "a genius, so to speak, for *sauntering*."

42

What the idea of sauntering concealed was just how programmatic Thoreau's daily walks could be—how little they resembled the wanderings of a true walker errant. Thoreau rarely walked simply for the sake of walking. Among other things, he was always adequately equipped. "Under his arm he carried an old music-book to press plants," Emerson recounts; "in his pocket, his diary and pencil, a spy-glass for birds, microscope, jack-knife, and twine. He wore straw hat, stout shoes, strong gray trousers, to brave scrub-oaks and smilax, and to climb a tree for a hawk's or a squirrel's nest." He also carried a sturdy stick, notched for measuring length and height, which was modeled after the post Robinson Crusoe had scored for measuring days and months. This was a man outfitted for a purpose.

"Walking" indicates that Thoreau usually set out in the same direction each morning, his handy compass settling "between west and south-southwest." He must have meant this more metaphorically than literally, since the territory he called Concord was a circle, not a straight line, and his walks covered every point of the compass. But it's a sign of Thoreau's singlemindedness. And it points to a far more important aspect of his walks. For Thoreau almost always began the day with something specific to discover or prove. He was given to such phrases as "I find by experiment" and "my theory was confirmed by observation," and it was as if each daily walk represented a hypothesis that needed to be tested or a task that needed to be completed. Many of his journal entries around the time he wrote "Walking" actually start with a destination: "Go to the Deep Cut"; "To Fair Haven Hill"; "To Goose Pond *via* E. Hosmer's"; "Up the river in a boat to Pelham's Pond with W.E.C." Though his reasons are often postponed, or said indirectly, or fragmented by other thoughts and events along the way, Thoreau usually makes it clear why he's chosen that particular place to go. He *might* have gone somewhere else that day, but he *needed* to go to the Deep Cut or Goose Pond.

Thoreau's writings prove that his private experiment at Walden was just the prologue to a life of investigation and problem solving. The philosopher Bruno Latour has noted that the etymology of "experiment" implies both "passing through" a trial of some sort and "coming out of it," having learned its lesson. Despite his own playful etymology, Thoreau's notion of sauntering was never meant to indicate idleness or errantry, but earned *information*. It was both a means of experimenting and a kind of experiment in its own right. As usual, Ellery Channing ("W.E.C." above) sums it up best, revealing both the rigor and the humor of Thoreau's enduring project: "Sometimes, where the matter was important, he carried with him a string of leading questions, carefully written, which he had the ability to get as skilfully answered,—though, if there was a theory to maintain, with a possible overlapping to his side of the argument. Ever on the search for knowledge, he lived to get information."

Thoreau believed that information essentially derived from the senses, explaining that "in my walks I would fain return to my senses." Maybe being ill for most of his life led him to closely monitor his body and his senses no matter what. As one of the Goncourt brothers said, sickness sensitizes us for observation. But as much as Thoreau railed against the "common sense" at times, his basic view of the world, and his basic view of Walden as his "proper nursery," was taken chapter and verse from the Bible of commonsense philosophy, John Locke's *An Essay concerning Human Understanding* (1689).

Locke famously introduces his notion of experience with a series of questions: "Let us then suppose the mind to be, as we say, white paper, void of all characters, without any ideas:—How comes it to be furnished? Whence comes it by that vast store which the busy and boundless fancy of man has painted on it with an almost endless variety? Whence has it all the *materials* of reason and knowledge? To this I answer, in one word, from EXPERIENCE." What Locke meant by "experience" was (1) "the Senses" that "convey into the mind several distinct perceptions of things," making it possible for us to "come by those *ideas* we have of *yellow, white, heat, cold, soft, hard, bitter, sweet*"; and (2) "the perception of the operations of our own mind within us"—our self-awareness of those ideas.

Locke's *Essay* is generally considered a cornerstone of empiricism and the scientific method. More than half a century earlier, Francis Bacon had called for the kind of observer who would have "unimpaired senses" and a "well-purged mind"—hoping to defy a tradition in which statements about the real world were verified by citing Ptolemy or Aristotle rather than studying the actual phenomena of nature. The *Essay* provided an epistemological justification for Bacon's approach. If the truth or existence of a natural phenomenon purportedly derived from the authority of an ancient text, what could be more threatening to that "scholastic" point of view than the authority of everyday experience? "God has not been so sparing to men to make them barely two-legged creatures," Locke says in the *Essay*, "and left it to Aristotle to make them rational."

Thoreau was alluding to Locke when he spoke of the "ancient scenes stamped on the tablet" of his memory. He was also alluding to Locke when he said how subdued he felt after the loss of his childhood senses. Taking both these things into account, I'm tempted to say that being so alert to what he'd gained from his senses made losing them that much worse. But Thoreau had a habit of exaggerating—in many ways it became his stock in trade—and while he may have yearned for the intensity of his first impressions, and tried to recapture them during his stay at Walden, he never viewed his senses as either static or lost forever. To say that they were would be to admit they were much too scant to experience the fleeting phenomena of nature. Thus: "We need pray for no higher heaven than the pure senses can furnish, a *purely* sensuous life. Our present senses are but the rudiments of what they are destined to become."

Statements like this occur throughout Thoreau's work. Plainly, he believed his senses could be more exact and poetic than they were, and far more open to experience. "What a faculty must that be which can paint the most barren landscape and humblest life in glorious colors!" he exclaims in the journal. "It is pure and invigorated senses reacting on a sound and strong imagination." This all-out love of the senses, along with the often humble reality he strove to picture, is just one of many things in Thoreau's writings which remind me of something the poet Czeslaw Milosz said in a 1999 interview: "We live in a world of languages—painting, music, cinema, poetry. But besides that language, there is a reality. That reality can be defined as everything that is not captured by our language but is directly perceived by our senses. I believe that reality is the great measure of art. It judges art."

Thoreau's perception of reality was so fluid and elated that I think it might be called synesthetic. This condition seems to be especially common if you're creative, because the neural pathways get crossed in one way or another and people begin to experience numbers, for example, as colors, or a sequence of musical notes as textures. From what I can tell, Thoreau often experienced synesthetic crossovers—like the time he wrote, "Every new flower that opens, no doubt, expresses a new mood of the human mind. Have I any dark or ripe orange-yellow thoughts to correspond? The *flavor* of my thoughts begins to correspond." In fact, one of the most notable features of Thoreau's work is the way he brings all of his senses into play, avidly depicting the wild and taunting laughter of a nearby loon; the sparkly, rippled glint of a pond brushed by breezes; the oddly passive feel of a fish in the hand; the sharp, invigorating taste of a plucked apple; the springlike smell of witch hazel in autumn. He never considered the senses singly, as if each were a room in a Victorian house.

Synesthesia may explain why Thoreau so readily resisted the inclination to think like a landscape painter. *Not* thinking this way was very unusual for the time, since Americans regularly bandied about the word "picturesque"—meaning that something was "like a picture" or "worthy of being pictured"—and had a habit of reducing nature to a picturesque, scenic view. Google almost any landscape by Thomas Cole or Frederic Edwin Church and you'll see that their paintings are inherently static, a matter of the perfect eye seeking the perfect view from the perfect spot. Picturesque travel books often included extremely precise directions so that others could stand exactly where the author had stood and experience exactly what he or she had singled out as the perfect view.

None of this squares with the way Thoreau came to describe the landscape. Once he came down from the summit in Maine, he walked away from the need to find a grand or ideal viewpoint, spending most of his time instead in the foot-sucking muck of swamps, the waist-high world of grasses, and the tangled, skin-piercing world of the huckleberry. He would stand for hours in a cold stream to observe the life of a frog and devote years to the study of how a single maple "faithfully husbanded its sap" and achieved "Mapledom." He would also walk in moonlight, or even darkness, guided more by scent or sound or the feel of the ground under his feet than by what he saw. At the very least, this meant that he gradually abandoned a stationary, strictly visual point of view in favor of a more mobile and multisensory perspective. More radically, it meant that he moved away from how nature *looked* to how it *worked*. Though he would take years to achieve it, Thoreau actually anticipated this trajectory in one of his first essays: "The true man of science will know nature better by his finer organization; he will smell, taste, see, hear, feel better than other men. His will be a deeper and finer experience. We do not learn by inference and deduction, and the application of mathematics to philosophy, but by direct intercourse and sympathy."

Thoreau wasn't just being wistful when he recalled both the "weariness" and the "refreshment" of his childhood senses. He was saying something important about the way he came to know nature. Weariness implies density, distance, speed, resistance, and all are aspects of what it means to learn by walking. Søren Kierkegaard reveled in the "gait of finitude," believing that a pedestrian approach to life's mysteries, its hard matter, its practical and moral limits, was the only way to create real mental traction. I'm inclined to say he was onto something, since almost by definition walking defies the law of inertia. Even the shortest walk is a form of departure as well as arrival. Certainly, it's a way to avoid marking time or moving in place—like riding in a wagon or a train during Thoreau's lifetime, and driving a car or surfing the web today. "We want to walk," Wittgenstein said, "so we need friction."

As we might expect, however, Thoreau's own art of walking created a very different relation to the land than the weariness that resulted from farming or other forms of physical labor. Farming in particular could be a numbing, bone-tiring life that left little room for curiosity or reflection, even during long winters, when there were still cows to milk and various other chores to do. Moreover, many farmers assumed there was a Manichean contrast between humans and nature—as if the land were an object, an enemy, a sphere to be leveled and ruled rather than sympathized with. Sadly, this antagonistic approach often made them the victims, not victors, of their labors. Missouri senator Thomas Hart Benton (a great-uncle of the twentieth-century muralist of the same name) was so demoralized by the year he spent farming that he gave it up and became a full-time politician.

Of course, Concord was also a county seat and a growing center of commerce while Thoreau was alive, so he didn't confine his criticism to farmers. Both in the journal and in "Walking" he pointedly confessed that he was "astonished at the power of endurance, to say nothing of the moral insensibility" of the merchants, lawyers, and other professionals who worked the nineteenth-century equivalent of nine-to-five every day, never leaving their offices or shops. He saw no difference between white-collar weariness and blue-collar weariness, especially since shopkeepers and office workers were even more alienated from the land by their labor.

Not surprisingly, Thoreau's fascination with waste strips and swamps turned out to be his most compelling *counter* friction to the sort of fatigue that normally defined life in Concord. Taken at face value, it's hard to think of anything more useless and tiring than slogging through a dense swamp, or anything more repugnant to a farmer or merchant. But here is Thoreau in his journal: "I remember gazing with interest at the swamps about those days and wondering if I could ever attain to such familiarity with plants that I should know the species of every twig and leaf in them." For him, fatigue represented something alive and gained, not something lost or inert. It was a way of wresting truth from falsehood, of turning boundaries into crossings, being into becoming. When the cultural theorist Paul Virilio writes that it's "the duration and extent of a physical fatigue that gives the world of tangible experience its measure," he leaves out half the story. The other half is the *nature* or *quality* of that physical fatigue. How else are we to take something like Francis Alÿs's *When Faith Moves Mountains* (2002), an artwork in which five hundred people shifted a sand dune about four inches by transferring the sand from one side of the dune to the other, one shovelful at a time? It was all about the inherent value of this outwardly Sisyphean task.

That Thoreau walked was less important than *how* he walked and what he walked *for*. This was especially clear during his moments of doubt or disappointment. Those who are hypersensitive to the natural world are also hypersensitive to the times it seems so resistant that it looks dead or out of reach—a rebuke to their ability to feel. "I wish I had a heart always open to such sensations," John Keats complains in one of his letters, "but there is no altering a Man's nature and mine must be radically wrong for it will lie dormant a whole Month." On occasion, Thoreau felt equally to blame, though he was quicker to regain his bearings. A journal entry from the summer of 1852 reads, "Nature has looked uncommonly bare and dry to me for a day or two. With our senses applied to the surrounding world we are reading our own physical and corresponding moral revolutions. Nature was so shallow all at once I did not know what had attracted me all my life. I was therefore encouraged when, going through a field this evening, I was unexpectedly struck with the beauty of an apple tree. The perception of beauty is a moral test." Only someone who saw the art of walking as a gait of resistance—a pressing interval in which he could "walk a mile into the woods bodily, without getting there in spirit"—would be likely to say this.

————

Resistance implies a slowing down or speeding up, a perceived thickness or thinness of matter, that was always part of the truth Thoreau discovered in nature. Virilio has also noted, more accurately, I believe, that "the truth of a phenomenon is always limited by the speed with which it emerges." However, within Thoreau's Concord, speed was a measure not only of distance and space but of the densities, the differences, and the connections that resulted from alert and directed walking. Thoreau was not just experimenting with the truth of walking itself, but with the truth that walking revealed. And what he found was that the area around Concord could be seen as something other than a series of compass points, or even a mere place in the usual sense. Here, too, it could be seen as a bioregion.

Before Thoreau really began to pay attention to Concord, its ten-mile radius made for a ready-made exercise in literary sensibility, but little more. Take the essay "Natural History of Massachusetts," a long and fairly romantic review of an official report on the state's fishes, reptiles, birds, plants, and harmful insects. Aside from all the metaphors Thoreau uses to spice things up, his main contribution is an allusion to Johann Wolfgang von Goethe's theory of the leaf. Two later essays, "A Walk to Wachusett" and "A Winter Walk," could have been written for an early incarnation of the Massachusetts Office of Travel and Tourism. A typical passage in "Wachusett" reads, "And here, on the top of a hill, in the shade of some oaks, near to where a spring bubbled out from a leaden pipe, we rested during the heat of the day, reading Virgil, and enjoying the scenery."

But as Thoreau began to study botany and zoology instead of just the classical poets, he gradually learned to identify the various plants and animals he encountered using Linnaeus's system of genus and species. Once he could identify these species, he felt more able to study their specific habits. And once he became acquainted with their habits, he felt more compelled to ask if all the individual species could be *linked* to one another within a larger system or habitat—one of the earliest examples of what we now call ecological thinking. A region he had only sketchily designated "a poem to be called Concord" began to emerge as a dense network of related yet specific phenomena and experiences: both a science *and* a poetry of connection.

In the manner of Zeno's best-known paradox, Thoreau kept halving his ignorance, developing smaller and smaller increments of knowledge, constantly refining his experience of nature while recognizing that he would never reach the limits of either himself or Concord. At one point, he was so amazed by the density of the world opening up to him that he marveled, "I wonder that I ever get five miles on my way, the walk is so crowded with events and phenomena." Indeed, density became a hallmark of his thinking. One of Emerson's daughters remarked later in life that Thoreau "never took us to walk with him, but sometimes joined us for a little way, if he met us in the woods on Sunday afternoon. He made those few steps memorable by showing us many wonders in so short a space."

All in all, this was yet another counter friction to the way people commonly experienced Concord. For the most part, Concord existed within a "surveyor's space"—that is, within the confines of the state, county, and individual property lines that Thoreau himself helped to measure and map. Shaped by the desire for greater profits, the logical course of surveyor's space is a greater uniformity. But Thoreau's "Concord" was a landscape of waxing roughness and difference, not smoothness and sameness. By walking out into the surrounding region, believing that "every man has to learn the points of the compass again as often as he awakes," he turned a uniform, known space—a space signified by what the philosopher Henri Lefebvre once termed the universal "dos and don'ts" of capitalism—into a new and unfamiliar world of natural wonders. "The aspects of the most simple object are as various as the aspects of the most compound," Thoreau notes. "Observe the same sheet of water from different eminences. When I have travelled a few miles I do not recognize the profile of the hills of my native village."

Admittedly, this growing awareness had certain drawbacks. By *in*creasing the detail and depth of his observations, Thoreau initially *de*creased his understanding of nature as a whole. Density made the world seem more partial, more separate, more disorderly. He found that being able to identify each species, for instance, was as much of a hindrance as a help. "How differently the poet and the naturalist look at objects!" he writes in a moment of apparent despair. "If you would make acquaintance with the ferns you must forget your botany." More generally, he concludes, "I fear that the character of my knowledge is from year to year becoming more distinct and scientific; that, in exchange for views as wide as heaven's cope, I am being narrowed down to the field of the microscope. I see details, not wholes nor the shadow of the whole."

He chose to deal with this problem by creating a relatively arbitrary and abstract whole—which is to say, the circle of ten miles' radius that became the "Concord" of his journal and his other writings after 1850 or so. Within these limits, Concord ceased to be a set of partial worlds. Instead, it became an entire world with missing parts. As Samuel Beckett pointed out, the distinction is mainly a question of degree—but it's an important degree, because Thoreau was able to slowly and systematically fill in the missing parts while still pointing to what he saw as a whole of some sort. I would add that Beckett came up with this distinction to show that many, even all *works of art* can represent a whole with missing parts. Think of *Walden*: a work as notable for its jumpy editing, its juxtaposed elisions and omissions, as William S. Burroughs's *Nova Express* (1964), Robert Rauschenberg's *Monogram* (1955–59), Jean-Luc Godard's *Breathless* (1960), or Takashi Murakami's astonishing painting, *In the Land of the Dead, Stepping on the Tail of a Rainbow* (2014).

"Walking" was first delivered as a lecture in 1851—more than ten years after Thoreau's first essay was published, and while he was in the middle of writing *Walden*. It's generally seen as a significant turning point in Thoreau's life, since a handwritten comment on the manuscript notes, "I regard this as a sort of introduction to all that I may write hereafter." But I believe the essay was yet another response to the colonial landscape and culture that had also prompted the temporary delay, the "speaking silence," Thoreau had sought at Walden. So I think he found it useful to traffic in what I would call the language of the double negative.

The tactic of doubling a negative to create a positive seems to have been repeatedly rediscovered as Americans struggled to separate themselves from England. Indeed, it's likely to arise in any dependent nation seeking sovereignty, at least in part because its people are both defensive and defiant at the same time. "Let us remember not to strive upwards too long," Thoreau advises, "but sometimes drop plumb down the other way, and wallow in meanness." That such "meanness" was especially important to Americans during the Revolutionary period is easy to understand.

Historian Martin Brückner has shown that prior to 1750 or so only the British used the word "American" for either the local population or the continent they occupied—and it was mainly to criticize the primitive conditions of colonial life. But during the Stamp Act crisis of 1764 things began to change. At first, the colonists simply turned the tables on the British by calling *themselves* American; then, in a more radical turn, they decided to tie their Americanness to the geographic figure of the continent itself. By the time Thomas Paine published *Common Sense* (1776), the continent had become both a crucial metaphor and a physical presence. Warning against "distinctions too limited for continental minds," Paine declared that "the sun never shined on a cause of greater worth. 'Tis not the affair of a city, a county, a province, or a kingdom, but of a continent—of at least one eighth part of the habitable globe."

The boldness of the colonists' move cannot be overstated. Even though most of the continent remained unexplored at the time—still considered "an howling wilderness" for the most part—the colonists deliberately opted to attach themselves to this amorphous interval of space. Rather than looking to those elements of colonial society that most resembled the stable and cultivated state of British landscape and culture, they instead chose to identify themselves with the very name, and the very territory, which had marginalized them as a political and geographical entity to begin with. Hoping to create a positive from what amounted to a double negative, the colonists in effect decided to negate the derogatory meaning of "America" by accentuating its supposedly most negative or uncertain aspects.

More than half a century after Paine, Emerson alluded to the tactic when he said, "self-reliance is precisely that secret, to make your supposed deficiency redundancy." So did the editor and critic Rufus Wilmot Griswold when he claimed that "most of the circumstances usually set down as barriers to aesthetical cultivation here are directly or indirectly advantageous." And it seems to have been a fundamental element of American nationalism during this period—of which the most important example is probably a report that the explorer John Frémont delivered to the U.S. Congress in 1842. Written to counter the belief that everything between the Mississippi River and the Rocky Mountains was an arid and barren desert, Frémont's report implied that the very elements that seemed to make the West most ugly in the eyes of Americans were actually the source of its greatest beauty. Basically, the report used one form of ugliness to offset another. More broadly, Frémont implied that what had often been portrayed as the ugliest region of the entire continent might be the source of *its* most distinctive beauty, too, the region that would finally render the American landscape equal to or better than Europe's in the eyes of Europeans and Americans alike.

Thoreau read Frémont's report about halfway through his stay at Walden, but he showed an awareness of the double negative almost from the beginning of his career. Remember that one of his earliest journal entries notes that "double a deformity is a beauty." Of course, this was little more than a passing thought at the time, not a call to arms. Again, I'd say that "A Walk to Wachusett," written in 1842, is typical of Thoreau's early writing. The essay recounts an excursion in which he consciously sets out in the footsteps of Samuel Johnson's Rasselas. He remarks that the landscape "reminds the traveller so often of Italy, and the South of France"; observes that the "uninterrupted light" of the moon is bright enough "to read Wordsworth distinctly"; and seems to have modeled the entire essay on Petrarch's celebrated ascent of Mont Ventoux in 1336. After returning from the trip to Maine, however, Thoreau began to amplify his senses and pare his language, gradually translating his writings into the systematic account of a landscape he had seen his whole life but "did not realize or appreciate." "Before I walked in the ruts of travel," he observed in the early stages of this metamorphosis, "now I adventured." "Walking" was the first account of this new adventure.

Rather than visualizing the American landscape as a grander or more inclusive version of European scenery, "Walking" spotlighted the sort of swampy, "zero panorama," "low profile" landscapes (as Robert Smithson would later call them) that Europeans and Americans alike had found so objectionable over the years. Thoreau decided to go little, not big, devoting himself to "the obscure life," "the barren fields," and "the smallest share of all things but poetic perception." "What you call barrenness and poverty," he remarks in 1856, "is to me simplicity." He had already begun to fill the journal with entries such as "I have been surprised to discover the amount of the various kinds of life which a single shallow swamp will sustain," and "I had no idea that there was so much going on in Heywood's meadow." Even at the time he wrote "Walking," he felt confident enough to boast that "English literature, from the days of the minstrels to the Lake Poets,—Chaucer and Spenser and Milton, and even Shakespeare, included,—breathes no quite fresh and in this sense wild strain. It is an essentially tame and civilized literature, reflecting Greece and Rome."

Needless to say, this was not just a criticism, but a *self*-criticism. Obviously, Thoreau was as eager as anyone at the time to broadcast in the language of Greece and Rome. When he wasn't quoting Hesiod or Virgil—or Ptolemy and Aristotle, for that matter—he was musing about approaching "the Roman age of manhood" and worrying about achieving "the life of the Greeks." That's why "Walking" should be seen as a declaration of independence from himself, from his fellow Americans, and from the long tradition of European literature, all at the same time. Among his contemporaries, only the writer Susan Fenimore Cooper and the painter George Inness showed such a fondness for backwater, tangential landscapes. But even they look half-hearted compared to what Thoreau chose to focus on and how he chose to portray it. In fact, we may still find it hard to accept some of the examples Thoreau lovingly cited to prove that even the lowest landscapes could set a new standard of beauty. A journal entry from 1851 reads, "Walk often in drizzly weather, for then the small weeds (especially if they stand on bare ground), covered with rain-drops like beads, appear more beautiful than ever,—the hypericums, for instance."

Thoreau drew our attention to such ignoble, everyday scenes specifically to extol the loveliness of America. Aware that evoking a European standard of art and beauty would only make his native environment look inferior or defensive by comparison, he instead elected to accentuate the elements that made it seem most out of the way or different. Like Frémont before him, one of Thoreau's lasting contributions to American landscape was his ability to present it as an object of beauty in its own right: marginal, unadorned, not too improved. He depicted a landscape whose beauty emerged from the utility or the necessary form of nature—from the beauty of "the thing itself, than which there is nothing more like it, no truer picture or account; which you cannot go farther and see."

Though the poet Rainer Maria Rilke once wrote that "almost all things beckon us to feeling," I find it hard to believe that without "Walking," or *Walden*, or many of Thoreau's other essays, we would have such classics of American natural history writing as Mary Austin's *The Land of Little*

Rain (1903), Aldo Leopold's *A Sand County Almanac* (1949), Marjorie Stoneman Douglas's *The Everglades: River of Grass* (1947), Annie Dillard's *Pilgrim at Tinker Creek* (1974), or John McPhee's *The Pine Barrens* (1968). All of these authors have acknowledged a debt to Thoreau's low-profile aesthetic, and all have added to the way this aesthetic countered the "learned ignorance"—the *docta ignorantia*, to secularize a term from theology—of a longstanding colonial tradition that had little use for anything as mundane or unimproved as small weeds standing on bare ground.

———

And so an essay that begins as a pilgrimage to the Holy Land finally ends less than ten miles outside of Concord in a swampy, "retired" meadow where "only a musquash looks out from his cabin" and "some little black-veined brook" meanders "slowly round a decaying stump." We should celebrate how oddly the arc of beauty bends in "Walking" and how doggedly Thoreau wanders to his Holy Land. For that matter, we should celebrate the way Thoreau inverts what *counts* as the Holy Land to begin with. But we can also enjoy the essay for the way it turns a labyrinth into a maze.

Borges was not being paradoxical, for once, when he spoke of a labyrinth that was a straight line. Examine most of the labyrinths laid into the floors of Medieval churches and you'll see that what looks like a nested series of different pathways is really an undeviating inward spiral to God and salvation—a miniature pilgrimage. A labyrinth is a single sentence, read from beginning to end, again and again. It's a litany meant to induce a loss of self, of thought, of anything but a growing nearness to God. But a maze—as Darwin or Wittgenstein might have said—is a kind of grammar, a set of rules that allows an infinite number of words to be combined in an infinite number of ways. Multiple and equally plausible pathways lead to an uncertain, and possibly nonexistent, end. One has to be alert, observant, aware of one's feelings, able to remember and compare. What if the Minotaur had kept moving instead of waiting for Theseus? The maze would still be a maze, something whole and distinct, but it would be a figure of constant departure, a novel and never-ending journey, not a destination or end point. It would also be, in Wittgenstein's words, "nothing out of the ordinary."

The same thing is true of Thoreau's sauntering. It was a way of setting out each day at the same time and in the same direction, only to swerve toward a location that could differ by as much as 180 degrees from the one that drew him the day before. The Deep Cut and Goose Pond only appeared to be end points. At a larger scale, and over a longer interval of time, they were more like forks in the road, nodes in the network. They could always be viewed with a different intention of the eye—appearing nearer to each other one day and farther away the next, depending on the sorts of questions Thoreau was asking himself at the time. Emerson got it exactly right when he noted in his journal that Thoreau "lives extempore, and brings today a new proposition as radical and revolutionary as that of yesterday, but different."

All of this leads me to say that the network or maze that Thoreau created by walking was basically a model of evolutionary change. According to the historian Michael North, Darwin came to believe that evolution was possible because change was "one of the innate tendencies of things" and *both* continuity and change derived from "the same physical mechanisms." North suggests that the mechanism of natural selection was actually a sophisticated new synthesis of many earlier theories of novelty—a novel idea of novelty. But Thoreau was quick to accept it because he already believed in at least a metaphysical form of orderly change. Very early in the journal he had concluded that "all things are in revolution it is the one law of nature by which order is preserved, and time itself lapses and is measured"; by the time he wrote "Walking," he had come to realize that the art of walking obeyed a similar law. That Thoreau set out each day with a different destination in mind, a new proposition to test, a fresh experience to explore—all within the same circle of ten miles' radius—showed that walking could do more than reveal the changing aspects of a stable and ordinary environment. It could be a form of change in its own right. The journal suggests that Thoreau sought to preserve the annual continuity of Concord by changing the nature and reach of each daily walk. To keep the maze intact, he multiplied its twists and turns. To insure that it remained whole, he never allowed it to be complete. Only by remaining open-ended could Concord retain a lasting identity.

If the journal entries are read in order—clearly the best indication of how Thoreau looked for something different in a humble, low-profile environment he saw every day—they gradually add up to a record of renewal and decay. "By the mediation of a thousand little mosses and fungi," he says at one point, "the most unsightly objects become radiant of beauty. There seem to be two sides to this world, presented us at the different times, as we see things in growth or dissolution, in life or death." Is it any surprise that Thoreau's favorite seasons of the year were spring and fall—routine intervals of rapid change? On the other hand, change itself didn't mean that things kept returning to the same starting point. Spring came to Concord every year, yes, but it signified a rediscovery of what was new about nature, not what was old. Though Thoreau claimed he could tell to the day when a particular species of plant would bloom, the day itself was always relative—subject to the mildness or harshness of the winter from one year to the next. When he also developed a time-line for autumn—describing the order in which each species of plant would turn color and shed its leaves—this Kalendar, as he called it, was just as relative.

As a matter of fact, the small differences Thoreau recorded year over year were the best indication of how nature changed *absolutely* as well as relatively. This is why his later work focused on such things as the succession of forest trees and the dispersal of seeds—"a sort of constant new creation" that gradually altered the ecology of the entire bioregion, resulting in an integrated, ever-branching network of newness. Maybe the people of Königsberg wanted their web of bridges to be a labyrinth, none crossed more than once, but Thoreau was happy to think of Concord as a maze, crossing and recrossing the same territory from a different point of the compass and a different intention of the eye every single day. Over the course of time, the counter friction created by his sauntering steadily transformed the existing semantics of colonialism and landscape painting into the grammar of American ecology.

CHAPTER 4

Seeing

The Museum of Modern Art has been a fixed point in my life ever since I moved to New York in 1971. Over the years I've seen the works of many friends and colleagues there. I've also seen a number of small, closely curated shows that made me reconsider an artist or movement, and more than a few of the splashy, blockbuster exhibitions that all museums feel compelled to mount these days—the sort of "must-see" events that are so crowded it's hard to see anything other than the crowd itself. Aside from the library, which has a large collection of artists' books and magazines, I can't say the museum has ever been that interested in *my* work or the work of the group known as Art & Language that I was part of for a while. But one day, as I was doing some research for a talk on political art, the librarian did make a point of coming out to meet me, and we spent some time discussing a short-lived but influential magazine I had helped to publish called *The Fox*.

Among the most famous paintings in the museum's collection is a large water-lily study by Claude Monet, loosely dated from the period between 1914 and 1926 when he completed most of these studies, and known specifically as *Reflections of Clouds on the Water-Lily Pond*. If memory serves, I initially saw the painting mounted on a long stretch of wall facing the museum's sculpture garden, where it was lit by natural light. Later, I remember seeing it on an interior, freestanding wall that you approached head-on from another room. Now it's hung in a relatively small room with two entrances, where you can see it either straight ahead or obliquely, off to your left.

I have to confess that until several years ago I had stopped looking at the painting. I considered it irrelevant to the kind of art I was interested in—little of which had to do with that era of painting—and I'd grown accustomed to passing it without a second glance. But as I was caught up in "The Ponds" chapter of *Walden* one day, I suddenly real-ized that the way Thoreau described the natural world had more than a passing resemblance to Monet's water-lily studies. A late journal en-try reads, "The philosopher for whom rainbows, etc., can be explained away never saw them. With regard to such objects, I find that it is not they themselves (with which the men of science deal) that concerns me; the point of interest is somewhere *between* me and them (i.e., the objects)." This need to inhabit an interval between the impression and the expression—*between himself and the world*—indicated that Thoreau had developed a very complex and modern way of seeing. But not until I made the connection to Monet's painting did I begin to appreciate the exact nature of his in-betweenness. At the same time, I began to see the painting itself in a new light—prompting several trips to the Modern just to study it.

Reflections of Clouds on the Water-Lily Pond is an enormous work, about six and a half feet high by forty-two feet long, dominated by a palette of cobalt blue, cobalt violet, viridian green, French ultramarine, emerald green, madder red, and lead white. It takes up an entire wall in the spotlit rectangular room, which also contains a smaller painting of water lil-ies on the opposite wall, two squarish, more easel-sized paintings titled *Agapanthus* and *The Japanese Footbridge* on the shorter end-walls, and two benches in the middle. No reproduction can do it justice, but anyone unable to see the painting in person can Google it by name to get an idea of what it looks like.

The painting is divided into three equal panels, joined side-to-side. Standing somewhat far away and reading it either left to right or right to left, the work as whole has the impassive quality of one of Jean-Luc Godard's signature tracking shots, with everything given the same em-phasis, the same degree of attention, allowing you to pick and choose what to focus on as you look. Monet has provided no center, no edge, no horizon, no vanishing point, and the painting can't be viewed from some ideal vantage point. Indeed, each of the panels is distinct in certain respects and each provokes a somewhat different response when looked at alone.

The one on the left is the most conventional. Painted in a fairly straightforward manner, the panel depicts several clumps of lily pads, a few with piercing vermilion flowers, floating in a realistic if rather vague space defined by the tilted surface of the pond. It's a space that allows you to get your bearings.

But jump to the middle panel and this tilted surface is almost lost. The only thing holding the eye in place are a few scattered lily pads and even they seem to be floating freely in clumps of clouds—a weirdly three-dimensional experience. All at once there seems to be little difference between water and sky. Are we looking down at a reflection in the water or up at a partly cloudy sky? Are the clouds slowly scudding by while the lily pads remain stationary? Why do the clouds seem so much more abstract than the floating pads—mere fluffs of white, mere allusions?

These ambiguities carry over to the third panel. Instead of reflecting the sky overhead the pond now seems bottomless, a dark and abstract void that may or may not indicate a cloud has abruptly obscured the sun. It's a lot like the either-or toggle of a window at night—all surface or mirror when a light in the room is on, completely transparent when it's off. But Monet includes *both aspects* of this toggle—not only from panel to panel, but within each panel. For next to a third cluster of lily pads, there appear to be some grassy or reedy tendrils waving slowly in the shallows of the pond, while its reddish, amorphous depths suddenly come to a bright vermilion point in the form of flower lying lushly on its surface. As with the other two panels, the eye is both anchored by the lily pads and set adrift. But what makes this cluster different from the other two is that the pads themselves are slightly elongated, slightly blurry, as if they might be moving along with the clouds. Whether this movement implies a kind of narrative spanning all three panels isn't clear. But, if it does, Godard again comes to mind. During one of the many interviews he gave over the years, Godard was asked if he felt his films should have a beginning, a middle, and an end. "Yes," he replied, "but not necessarily in that order."

Godard's cheeky response is a reminder that we usually think of art as being transparent. For the most part, we just focus on *what* the artist seems to be saying or showing, paying little or no attention to the ways in which that meaning depends on *how* it's being said or shown. But Monet's water-lily studies deliberately draw attention to themselves *as* paintings. Like many other modernist works, they force us to see that they're both an object and a form of representation, both real and virtual. What Wittgenstein said of philosophy—that it's "a fight against the fascination which forms of expression exert on us"—was also true of modernism.

As you move closer to Monet's painting, its illusionistic realism and depth slowly give way to the sheer materiality of canvas and paint. A lily pad becomes a few strokes of emerald green, a cloud becomes a whirl of lead white, and the tilted surface of the pond becomes the flat surface of the canvas. Soon you begin to notice that even the most watery, transparent effects are the result of Monet laying on the paint thick and dry. You also notice that some of the areas that read as if they're deeper in space turn out to be built up—a lumpy, honeycombed crust of pigments dragged over pigments. And some of the areas that seem most heavily worked on when viewed close up seem the most formless or unfinished from a distance. To be sure, this spasmodic switch in scale and perspective is true of almost any painting viewed closely enough. A painting *is* a painting no matter what. But Monet wants us to *pay attention* to his thickly brushed surface even as we look past it or through it to the image it represents. He wants us to appreciate that a picture must be always pictured—that it's not an innocent, transparent object, but a contrived, double-edged one.

This is basically what *Reflections of Clouds on the Water-Lily Pond* comes down to: a series of double-sided views. Everything in the painting is meant to mirror something else and everything is meant to make us both look and reflect on the act of looking at the same time. "Think twice before you think," e. e. cummings once said—which in Monet's case translates as "look twice before you see." Not to look twice—not to look from both sides at once—is to blunt the very thing that makes *Reflections of Clouds on the Water-Lily Pond* so radical. And the same thing applies to Thoreau's way of seeing.

Thoreau's most explicit and wide-ranging comments about seeing can be found in the essay "Autumnal Tints." From the journal, we know that he'd just finished reading John Ruskin's *The Elements of Drawing* (1857), a book strongly influenced by John Locke's belief that the mind traffics in visual images, and one of the texts Monet himself studied forty years later. Though it isn't clear how directly Ruskin's book influenced either man, the work they unknowingly read in common may explain why "Autumnal Tints" anticipates many aspects of Monet's water-lily studies. We see this most acutely toward the end of the essay, where Thoreau refers to what he calls a "different intention of the eye"—a notion that pictures the basic act of seeing as a fluctuating interval, a visual toggle.

Sometimes it's hard to tell whether "a different intention of the eye" means that Thoreau is seeing *two different* objects, as Nietzsche or Borges might have suggested, or the *same* object in two different ways. While trying to figure this out, I was especially drawn to Borges's "Funes the Memorious"—the labyrinthine story of a man who, among other things, has trouble understanding why "the dog at three fourteen (seen from the side) should have the same name as the dog at three fifteen (seen from the front)."

However, I would say Thoreau's point of view is more like the familiar gestalt puzzle in which a single black-and-white image appears as either a vase or the profiles of two people face-to-face, but never both at once. Certainly, that's the picture that comes to mind when he admits, "I have found that it required a different intention of the eye, in the same locality, to see different plants, even when they were closely allied, as *Juncaceae* and *Gramineae*: when I was looking for the former, I did not see the latter in the midst of them." Though this might seem like he's seeing Juncaceae (rushes) as one object and Gramineae (grasses) as another, what he's really portraying is an oscillation between two different aspects of a *single locality*—which is exactly what it's like to look at *Reflections of Clouds on the Water-Lily Pond.* Indeed, there's an obvious comparison between Monet's painting and a description of Thoreau and his brother slowly floating downstream in *A Week on the Concord and Merrimack Rivers*: "We notice that it required a separate intention of the eye, a more free and abstracted vision, to see the reflected trees and the sky, than to see the river bottom merely; and so are there manifold visions in the direction of every object, and even the most opaque reflect the heavens from their surface. Some men have their eyes naturally intended to one and some to the other object."

A number of commentators over the years have tried to explain Thoreau's double-sided view. More often than not, they've reduced this doubleness to a conflict between poetry and science or subjectivity and objectivity. And it's easy to see why. For instance, right after indicating how hard it was to see two different plants in the same locality, Thoreau goes on to remark, "How much more, then, it requires different intentions of the eye and of the mind to attend to different departments of knowledge! How differently the poet and the naturalist look at objects!" I've already noted a journal entry from 1859, "If you would make acquaintance with the ferns you must forget your botany"; another, from 1860, reads, "No one but a botanist is likely to distinguish nicely the different shades of green with which the open surface of the earth is clothed." These and many other passages in his writings suggest that Thoreau liked to favor one side or other of the equation or to treat them as two equal and opposing variables.

Yet once again I'd say that Thoreau more typically occupied an interval *between* poetry and science, subjectivity and objectivity. He wasn't Hamlet, endlessly dithering, endlessly unable to make up his mind. Nor was he Alexander the Great, decisively cutting the Gordian Knot. He was neither and both. Yes, he usually viewed poetry and science as distinct points of view; yes, he treated them as equal and offsetting elements; but he never reduced one to the other, never settled on one or the other, and never viewed them as opposites. They were a gestalt, not a polarity—and thus equivalent to the rather peculiar and ambiguous object known as *Reflections of Clouds on the Water-Lily Pond*.

No one has written more clearly or concisely about gestalts than Wittgenstein. His masterpiece, the *Philosophical Investigations* (1953), contains a short section on gestalts that comes as close as anything I can think of to explaining Thoreau's own philosophy of seeing. For some reason, Wittgenstein chose not to use the vase-profile gestalt or the one popularly known as "my wife and my mother-in-law" (both of which have delighted the painter Jasper Johns in recent decades). Instead he chose the "puzzle-picture" of a duck-rabbit that had appeared in a nineteenth-century German humor magazine. It's exactly the same kind of double-sided figure as the other two—as you can see if you Google it—and Wittgenstein utilized the figure to illustrate the difference between what he called "seeing" and "seeing-as."

Many people will look at a picture of the duck-rabbit and say, "I see a duck." Many others will look at it and say, "I see a rabbit." If two people are standing side by side, and one sees only a duck, while the other sees only a rabbit, they may stare at each other in disbelief or mistrust. I have a *New Yorker* cartoon by Paul Noth pinned to my wall which shows two

Herbert Wendell Gleason, *Reflections in "smooth vernal lake" by village,—downstream from the Bridge, April 15, 1918.* Courtesy of Concord Free Public Library.

armies facing off against each other, each holding up pennants with exactly the same image of a duck-rabbit, and a caption that reads, "There can be no peace until they renounce their Rabbit God and accept our Duck God." Both sides are suffering from what Wittgenstein called "seeing" or "continuous aspect seeing."

"Seeing-as" is something that happens if we unexpectedly perceive that a duck might also be *seen as* a rabbit or vice versa, which Wittgenstein refers to as "noticing an aspect" to set it apart from the stasis of seeing something the same way all the time. The image of the duck-rabbit hasn't changed, but the way we see it has. Suddenly, it has two aspects instead of one—a doubleness we didn't perceive before, but do now, because we're no longer simply reporting what we see but acknowledging that a single object can be seen as *either* a duck or a rabbit. Even if we were to say, knowing that such a double-sided figure exists, "I see a duck-rabbit," it

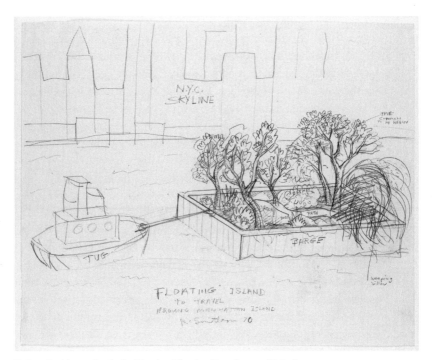

Robert Smithson, *Study for Floating Island to Travel around Manhattan Island*, 1970. Pencil on paper, 19 x 24 in. Courtesy of James Cohan, New York. Art © Holt-Smithson Foundation/Licensed by VAGA, New York, N.Y.

would still be just a simple report if we didn't go on to say, "Now I see it as a duck and now I see it as a rabbit." Without an awareness of this oscillation—as if the object has changed before our eyes without actually changing—we lack the distance and doubleness that fascinated both Wittgenstein and Thoreau. One of Thoreau's journal entries reads, "Such doubleness and distance does sight improve."

All of this is to say that Wittgenstein's figure of the duck-rabbit is neither a polarity nor a "reconciliation of opposites"—notions critical to Samuel Taylor Coleridge's theory of poetry, and the inspiration for many accounts of Thoreau's supposed split between poetry and science. A duck is not a mirror image of a rabbit, not even a chiral mirroring, like the right and left hands, say. Nor is "duck" an antonym of "rabbit," like top and bottom, or heavy and light, apathy and ardor. Nor do they somehow represent opposing categories of animals. Really, they're not opposites at all. They're just *different* from each other—different aspects of a single object or locality, each requiring a different intention of the eye. And yet we only perceive them as different if we choose to inhabit the sort of interval that allows us to continuously toggle between them, continuously see them *as* a duck or a rabbit, *as* Juncaceae or Gramineae, *as* a reflection or a river bottom, rather than just fixating on one or the other. I'm reminded of the nervous systems of certain insects, which seem to include both a sense of gravity and a sense of light, allowing them to locate the vertical in either sunlight or darkness.

Thoreau never regarded the disparity between poetry and science as a conflict between two opposing points of view, each picturing a separate and different object. On the contrary, he saw it as two different aspects of a single object. That's what he meant when he said, "How differently the poet and the naturalist look at objects!" It's why he never abandoned one point of view for the other, never reduced one to the other, but spent his entire life shifting back and forth. Perceived separately and alone, each made nature seem still and one-dimensional; perceived as a whole, nature became an extremely complex, equivocal, and continuously evolving object. As in Borges's imaginary Tlön—where "they do not say 'moon,' but rather 'round airy-light on dark' or 'pale-orange-of-the-sky'"—there can even be "objects composed of two terms, one of visual, and another of auditory character: the color of the rising sun and the faraway cry of a bird." And thus in *Walden*: "Innumerable little streams overlap and interlace one another, exhibiting a sort of hybrid product, which obeys half way the law of currents, and half way that of vegetation."

Starting with "The Ponds"—the ninth of eighteen chapters in *Walden*, and the hinge on which it swings from being a work of social commentary to something like a natural history of Concord—Thoreau developed a distinctive way of writing that alternated between poetry and science. Up to this point most of his natural history writings had been elaborated as excursions. "A Winter Walk," "A Walk to Wachusett," and "Natural History of Massachusetts" all seem to have been modeled on Goethe's *Italian Journey*, published in 1816–17. But in "The Ponds" he began to juxtapose a sometimes subtle, sometimes flagrant lyricism with a steadily more sophisticated and original empiricism. In the opening paragraphs of the chapter there is a description that might just as well apply to *Reflections of Clouds on the Water-Lily Pond*: "Walden is blue at one time and green at another, even from the same point of view.

Lying between the earth and the heavens, it partakes of the color of both. Viewed from a hill-top it reflects the color of the sky; but near at hand it is of a yellowish tint next the shore where you can see the sand, then a light green, which gradually deepens to a uniform dark green in the body of the pond."

"Autumnal Tints" is filled with poetic yet closely observed descriptions like this. The essay as a whole shifts back and forth between a systematic chronology of autumnal changes and a protracted examination of beauty and seeing. What's true of the entire essay is also true of its parts. Consider Thoreau's description of a scarlet oak:

> Stand under this tree and see how finely its leaves are cut against the sky,— as it were, only a few sharp points extending from a midrib. They look like double, treble, or quadruple crosses. They are far more ethereal than the less deeply scolloped Oak-leaves. They have so little leafy *terra firma* that they appear melting away in the light, and scarcely obstruct our view. The leaves of the very young plants are, like those of full grown Oaks of other species, more entire, simple, and lumpish in their outlines; but these, raised high on old trees, have solved the leafy problem. Lifted higher and higher, and sublimated more and more, putting off some earthiness and cultivating more intimacy with the light each year, they have at length the least possible amount of earthy matter, and the greatest spread and grasp of skyey influences. There they dance, arm in arm with the light.

Equally representative is Thoreau's description of three herons, taken from the period in which the journal became a daily record of his wanderings, including those with Ellery Channing (the second party in "us"):

> Scared up three blue herons in the little pond close by, quite near us. It was a grand sight to see them rise, so slow and stately, so long and limber, with an undulating motion from head to foot, undulating also their large wings, undulating in two directions, and looking warily about them. With this graceful, limber, undulating motion they arose, as if so they got under way, their two legs trailing parallel far behind like an earthy residuum to be left behind. They are large, like birds of Syrian lands, and seemed to oppress the earth, and hush the hillside to silence, as they winged their way over it, looking back toward us. It would affect our thoughts, deepen and perchance darken our reflections, if such huge birds flew in numbers in our sky. Have the effect of magnetic passes. They are few and rare. Among the birds of celebrated flight, storks, cranes, geese, and ducks. The legs hang down like a weight which they raise, to pump up as it were with its wings and convey out of danger.

What we find over and over again in these and other passages is that whenever Thoreau veers in the direction of pure lyricism, he suddenly stops short with a very detailed and informed observation. And whenever he's on the verge of being too dry and matter of fact, he quickly swerves in a more emotional and aesthetic direction. As with any puzzle-picture, neither side dictates or prevails. Instead, by oscillating between them, Thoreau always forces us to see both sides at once. Now we see it as poetic, now we see it as scientific—different aspects of the same complex object. The undulating legs of a heron can both pump it into flight and suggest the "earthy residuum to be left behind." It's all a matter of how we look at things, including how we look at the act of looking.

———————

Thoreau's emphasis on the different aspects of nature is important because he was far more interested in the interval between the familiar and the unfamiliar—the interval of *recognition*—than he was in the difference between poetry and science per se. One journal entry reads, "The question is not what you look at, but what you see." Another reads, "I am interested in an indistinct prospect, a distant view, a mere suggestion often, revealing an almost wholly new world to me. I rejoice to get, and am apt to present, a new view."

Wittgenstein was just as fascinated by the possibilities of a new or disoriented view. Toward the end of the *Investigations* he tells us, "A philosophical problem has the form: 'I don't know my way about.'" He has already identified this feeling of disorientation with a need to notice the different aspects of things: "You approach from *one* side and you know your way about; you approach the same place from another side and no longer know your way about." Since the familiar might be defined as a form of "continuous aspect seeing," he seems to be saying that we have to risk the state of being lost or disoriented to spot the *un*familiar that always exists within the familiar. "The aspects of things that are most important for us are hidden because of their simplicity and familiarity. (One is unable to notice something—because it is always before one's eyes.)"

Darwin was undoubtedly right when he said that we feel most strongly about the things we already know. But both Wittgenstein and Thoreau looked at what we already know with a different intention of the eye, alert to what Wittgenstein called the "possibilities" of phenomena more than phenomena as such. To seek such possibilities could mean something as simple as walking backwards, or in moonlight instead of sunlight, or with the head inverted or inclined. "What shall we make of the fact that you have only to stand on your head a moment to be enchanted with the beauty of landscape?" Thoreau wonders. In fact, this sort of voluntary alienation of the familiar is probably typical of artists and writers. Auguste Rodin resorted to a version of standing on his head when he used the way a mirror reverses everything to check if some of his more realistic sculptures were also beautiful and interesting purely as spatial forms. The poet Vladimir Mayakovsky believed that "the new can be not some object that is still unknown to everyone in our grey-haired world but a change in looking at relationships between objects."

For Thoreau, the familiar was almost always a journey into the unfamiliar. He hailed the poet "who describes the most familiar object with a zest and vividness of imagery as if he saw if for the first time, the novelty consisting not in the strangeness of the object, but in the new and clearer perception of it." In "Autumnal Tints" he says that "objects are concealed from our view, not so much because they are out of the course of our visual ray as because we do not bring our minds and eyes to bear on them; for there is no power to see in the eye itself, any more than in any other jelly. We do not realize how far and widely, or how near and narrowly, we are to look. The greater part of the phenomena of Nature are for this reason concealed from us all our lives." An earlier journal entry reads, "If I invert my head this morning and look at the woods in the horizon, they do not look so far off and elysian-like as in the afternoon. If I am not mistaken, it is late in the afternoon that the atmosphere is in such a state that we derive the most pleasure from and are most surprised by this experiment." Given these sorts of insights and conjectures, is it any wonder that *Walden* continues to amaze us? What could be more experimental than the *un*familiar picture of a humble, barely wooded pond that emerges in its pages?

Thoreau's style is especially interesting. Echoing an obsession with the "plain style" of speech and writing so important to the Puritans—Puritan ministers in particular—he occasionally said that he'd like to "return to the primitive analogical and derivative senses of words." "Plain speech is always a desideratum," he writes in an early journal entry. "If the words were sufficiently simple and answering to the thing to be expressed, our sentences would be as blossoming as wreaths of evergreen and flowers." But as he came to know nature better, it was as if this side of his thinking became two-sided, too. Long before Wittgenstein made it a cornerstone of the *Philosophical Investigations*, Thoreau was acutely aware that the limits of his world were defined by the limits of his language.

Inevitably, Thoreau sought an interval between words and things, not the things themselves. Words might, like the railroad tracks next to Walden, have a tangential relation to things, approaching closer and closer. They might also have an analogical or metaphorical relation to each other. But the interval between them could never shrink to zero. Thus, H. Daniel Peck, one of the many excellent literary historians who've studied Thoreau in recent decades, has noted that "The Ponds" chapter of *Walden* was written, not in a single, elemental style, but in a wide and boisterous array of styles. Peck's exemplary list includes the empirical, the "scenic or pastoral," the "extravagantly metaphorical," the "legendary associative," the allegorical, the lyrical, and the "reverie which quickly gives way to loss"—transforming "the lyrical into the elegiac." Since each is associated with a different aspect of the pond, style itself becomes an aspect of Thoreau's ongoing effort to expose the unfamiliar within the familiar. The possibilities of language are equated with the possibilities of nature. Each is an aspect of the other.

Though it may seem paradoxical, the alluring "life in nature" that so tempted Thoreau also implied a basic separation from nature—a constant negotiation within the sphere of language and culture. Thoreau believed that nature was physically and morally equivalent to humanity. But he wasn't looking for some absolute identity that would eliminate human consciousness altogether. During his daily walks around Concord, questions about nature went hand in hand with questions about the way he chose to write about nature. Indeed, virtually his entire life after his stay at Walden can be seen as a detailed examination of nature's relationship to language—leading him to conclude that "nature will be my language full of poetry." On the other hand, no one who believed that "poetry puts an interval between the impression and the expression" viewed language as transparent. Maybe Thoreau wouldn't have gone as far as Arthur Schopenhauer, who argued that people never really know either "the sun or the earth," merely "an eye that sees a sun" and "a hand that feels an earth," because "the surrounding world exists only as representation," but sometimes his philosophy of language comes pretty close. A journal entry from 1853 reads, "Is it not as language that all natural objects affect the poet? He sees a flower or other object, and it is beautiful or affecting to him because it is a symbol of his thought, and what he indistinctly feels or perceives is matured in some other organization. The objects I behold correspond to my mood."

Thoreau wrote to disrupt the everyday habits of seeing. "Let your walks now be a little more adventurous," he advises his readers near the end of "Autumnal Tints." "If about the last of October, you ascend any hill in the outskirts of our town, and probably of yours, and look over the forest, you may see—well, what I have endeavored to describe. All this you surely *will* see, and much more, if you are prepared to see it,—if you *look* for it." Though this may sound a bit pompous, Thoreau wasn't really asking others to see what he saw, but to stop seeing what they expected to see and really look for themselves. It was more a matter of *how* they saw than *what* they saw. Based on his own experience, he believed that looking with a different intention of the eye would transform the simple, ingrained habit of seeing into the far more self-conscious act of seeing-as. If nothing else, this shift would eliminate the sort of apathy or disappointment that often lies in wait for those who have an image of a place in mind before they see it.

When Margaret Fuller first encountered Niagara Falls in 1843, she said that her head was so stuffed with preexisting images that she stood on the bridge to Goat Island and said to herself, "ah, yes, here is the fall, just as I have seen it in picture." But after noting that the sight struck her "*well enough*," she began to wonder why it didn't provoke a stronger, more "surpassing" emotion. Gradually she realized that it was because she "thought only of comparing the effect on my mind with what I had read and heard"—a comparison in which the real thing always fell short. Not until she experienced the "poetical indefiniteness" of the falls at night, in a spot where "no gaping tourists loitered," did she feel the full force and grandeur of the scene. But, having shown such a faltering inclination to see things differently herself, she still ends her account on a regretful note: "Happy were the first discoverers of Niagara, those who could come unawares upon this view and upon that, whose feelings were entirely their own."

During the 1870s and '80s, many of those who traveled to Yellowstone experienced a somewhat similar letdown. In this case, they had been inspired by a single amazing image: Thomas Moran's *The Grand Canyon of the Yellowstone*. Moran had created the monumental, eight-by-twelve-foot painting in 1872, several months after the Yellowstone region was set aside as the country's first national park, and it quickly became the best-known symbol of the new park and a national icon in its own right. Not only was the painting viewed by hundreds of thousands of people when it toured all the major East Coast cities, but it was the first "pure" landscape bought by Congress and placed in the Senate lobby.

Yet once those who were familiar with Moran's work saw Yellowstone for themselves, they realized the artist had cobbled together three separate and distinct views, combining the V-shaped canyon, the tumbling Lower Falls, and the geyser basin beyond in a way that made it impossible to actually locate his supposed vantage point on the canyon rim. Moran freely admitted to this aesthetic sleight of hand, while insisting that the painting as a whole was "strictly true to pictorial Nature." That wasn't how some early visitors to the park saw it, however. Contrary to Fuller's experience at Niagara Falls, they were disappointed to discover they *couldn't* say to themselves, "Ah, yes, here is the canyon, just as I have seen it in picture."

It seems especially strange, then, that the park has now designated a specific spot on the canyon rim as Artist's Point and mounted a laminated reproduction of Moran's painting there. Anyone comparing the painting to what it depicts can see that both it and Artist's Point are an outright fiction, a virtual reality. I found this out for myself a few years ago when I made a detour to the park while researching a book on John Frémont. Standing before the washed-out reproduction, trying to reconcile it with the scene beyond, I noticed that Moran had subtly lowered both the rim of the canyon and the height of the distant plateau to create a nonexistent view of the Norris Geyser Basin to the west. He'd also included a dark, rocky outcropping on the right that was actually behind him as he faced the falls and located on a different part of the rim altogether.

Not that any of this seemed to matter by the time I visited the park. Even if people actually bothered to look at the picture—and most didn't when I was there—I doubt it either electrified or disturbed their own experience of the park. At most, the painting seemed to be a historical curiosity, something to be included *in* a picture of the park, not the very picture of the park itself. My own impression was that the park had become more like a huge outdoor museum than anything else, with people following a lengthy hourglass-shaped loop from Mammoth Hot Springs to the Lower Falls, as if they were moving from one painting to the next. By stringing together Moran's iconic elements linearly, one after the other, the park had indirectly created a three-dimensional version of the painting that obviated any need to see all three elements at the same time.

Contrast this to how we still think of Carleton Watkins's *Yosemite Valley from the Best General View* (1866), a work that helped to make the Yosemite region famous in the 1860s and has been widely reproduced ever since. Watkins took his "mammoth-plate" photograph six years before Moran painted the *Grand Canyon*, but he used the same approach, wedging the most emblematic features of the *U*-shaped valley into a single frame. Moran must have been aware of the picture, if only because the photographer William H. Jackson accompanied him to Yellowstone and Jackson was familiar with it. Still, there was an obvious difference between the two images: whereas Moran's view of Yellowstone was strictly virtual, Watkins's view of Yosemite was not. Visitors to Yosemite *could* duplicate the photographer's vantage point high above the valley, *could* stand where he'd stood, *could* say to themselves, "Ah, yes, here is the valley, just as I have seen it in picture."

In fact, this still seems to be what many people are looking for when they come to Yosemite: the chance to see for themselves the various *pictures* that have inspired them to see the park in the first place. I'm sure many of us have found ourselves at one of the roadside overlooks, either willing or unwilling collaborators, as two or three people spilled out of a car or a large group of people filed out of a bus, hurriedly snapped a few pictures of themselves in front of the photogenic scene and then left without a backward glance. There has been an effortless, almost "natural" progression from Watkins's *Yosemite Valley from the Best General View* to Ansel Adams's *Yosemite Valley, Yosemite National Park* (1934), to the commercial postcard, the snapshot, and the selfie. We seem to have reached the point where liking something "well enough" is good enough. A popular website says of the short but steep hike to Inspiration Point, the spot where Watkins took his photo, "The main purpose of nearly anyone hiking this trail is to photograph Yosemite Valley." Moreover, people don't just want to photograph the valley, they want to duplicate

Watkins's or Adams's photos of it. Thus, the website continues, "There's only one really prime spot for photography, so if there's anyone else on the trail, you'll be headed to the same patch of rock."

It's harder than ever these days to escape preexisting, prepackaged images. We wander in a rampantly visual world, with thousands of familiar images lodged in our heads, many of them of things we'll never see firsthand. The great cultural theorist Walter Benjamin was among the first to recognize that photography would create such a boundless universe of images that a single instant of history could symbolize an entire era—prompting him to observe that history decays into pictures, not stories. The same thing is true of nature. If we've come to see Yosemite and Yellowstone as little more than excuses for a photograph, it's mainly because we think of *nature itself* that way. I can't seem to forget Robert Smithson's harsh pronouncement: "most people who don't look too hard tend to see the world through postcards and calendars so that that affects their idea of what they think nature should be rather than what it is." Even Herbert Gleason's admirable photographs of Walden—most of them taken between 1899 and 1920, and fairly innovative at the time for their low-key approach—have come to look like clichés. When the Sierra Club published a series of consciousness-raising coffee-table books in the early 1960s, the first thing they came up with was *In Wildness Is the Preservation of the World* (1962), an inspirational tribute to Thoreau lavishly illustrated by the photographs of Eliot Porter, which were mostly colorful, calendar versions of Gleason's black-and-white photos of Walden Pond.

This limited, antecedent sort of view is precisely what Thoreau wanted to avoid. When he says that "we are as much as we see," he doesn't mean as much as we *already* see or simply *expect* to see. Instead, he believed the act of seeing should effectively be an act of *un*seeing by seeing differently. "I have been surprised to discover the amount and the various kinds of life which a single shallow swamp will sustain," he says in the journal, giving voice to a sense of wonder that would only grow as he paid more and more attention to the everyday world. In the end, Thoreau's greatest legacy may be that he thought the ordinary, unassuming landscape of Concord and Walden Pond was not just worth looking at but worth looking at closely and with reverence his entire life—each day a new walk, each day a new world, each day both more familiar and more unfamiliar at the same time. Thoreau was the first to truly *recognize* this landscape and the first to make us recognize it, too.

CHAPTER 5

Nature

Around 1520, a Spanish historian named Pietro Martire d'Anghiera wrote a striking description of an animal unknown to Europeans until Christopher Columbus returned from one of his voyages to the New World. Translated into the English of the day, d'Anghiera's portrayal reads, "Amonge these trees is fownde that monstrous beaste with a snowte lyke a foxe, a tayle lyke a marmasette, eares lyke a batte, handes lyke a man, and feete lyke an ape, bearing her whelpes aboute with her in an outward bellye much lyke unto a greate bagge or purse." More than anything, this baffled account indicates how hard it was for d'Anghiera and other Europeans to find a place in their natural world for the first marsupial they'd ever seen, the common possum. Unable to think of the possum as an animal in its own right, Europeans effectively turned it into a small-scale version of the hybrid creatures that populated Greek and Roman myths. And they seemed no less bewildered once the New World actually became their home.

I came across d'Anghiera's description in Susan Scott Parrish's excellent study of seventeenth- and eighteenth-century American science. Parrish shows how the Puritans, in particular, developed an obsessive interest in the oddest or most terrifying aspects of the new environment they encountered—a bias that helped to shape their perception of New England as "an howling wilderness." Cotton Mather's *Curiosa Americana* (1712–24) was a compendium of what he and others called "prodigies" or "portents," including mermen, two-headed snakes, and buried giants. Mather considered prodigies a sign of God's presence in New England: an indication that God favored the Puritans enough to offer them a refuge, but wanted to test their faith and devotion by forcing them to overcome its most terrifying aspects. Yet Mather also believed that natural oddities and events helped to define the peculiar character of New England—its *genius loci*, or spirit of place. His interest in Isaac Newton and Robert Boyle led him to closely study and record these natural phenomena *as* natural phenomena rather than just religious omens. Even more surprisingly, he believed in the germ theory of disease and was among the first persons anywhere to devise an experiment in plant hybridization.

Thoreau's own reputation as a scientist has waxed and waned over the years. Among those who knew him in Concord, on his home turf, he was generally considered a scientific genius—which is to say, someone completely in touch with nature. Bronson Alcott called him "a sylvan soul" and "a genius of the natural world." Hawthorne wrote, "Nature, in return for his love, seems to adopt him as her especial child, and shows him secrets which few others are allowed to witness." Emerson, alluding to Charles Wilkes's *Narrative of the United States Exploring Expedition, during the Years 1838, 1839, 1840, 1841, 1842,* said he "would have been competent to lead a 'Pacific Exploring Expedition.'"

But when Thoreau made three separate trips to the interior of Maine, and three to the beaches of Cape Cod, he seemed on shakier ground. A Maine resident named Fanny Hardy Eckstorm accused Thoreau of being more wrong than right about her home state—and "most wrong upon his points of pride" as a land surveyor, since he made a lot of errors in estimating distance, area, and the speed of rivers. "Even when he says that his surveyor's eye thrice enabled him to detect the slope of the current, he magnifies his office," she noted tartly. "Any woman who can tell when a picture hangs straight can see the slant of the river in all these places." Another woman, the daughter of a Thoreau family relative who lived on Cape Cod, recounted that because he "gauged everything by his beloved Concord River," Thoreau seriously miscalculated how fast the tide rose in Plymouth Harbor and would have drowned one summer day if a small fishing boat hadn't happened by.

Neither of these criticisms was as severe as John Burroughs's, however. Ridiculing Thoreau's *greatest* point of pride—his knowledge of the plants and animals around Concord—Burroughs declared that while Thoreau "was up and out at all hours of the day and night, and in all seasons and weathers," he ultimately failed "to make any new or valuable contribution to natural history." Burroughs blamed this failure squarely on Thoreau's "speculative," literary attitude, claiming "his mood was subjective rather than objective." Since Thoreau himself admitted as much sometimes, this accusation has stuck to him ever since. The modern botanist Ray Angelo has gone even further than Burroughs, adopting the rather condescending view that Thoreau *never* intended "to add to the body of botanical knowledge," merely "to distinguish more clearly the textures with which Nature clothed his native town"—as if he were all style, no substance.

Only in recent decades have botanists and biologists either looked past Thoreau's literary pyrotechnics or gleaned how much his extravagant style actually served his empirical eye, learning to appreciate what the ecologist Gary Paul Nabhan has called his "remarkably acute ecological insights into plant-animal interactions." Singling out Thoreau's interest in seed dispersal, Nabhan notes that he was the first Anglo-American naturalist to be influenced by Darwin's theory of natural selection and the first to broach "issues in plant population biology and coevolution that did not become fully articulated in evolutionary ecology until the early 1970s."

The same thing could be said of Thoreau's methodology. Almost everyone else studying seed dispersal at the time focused on botanical *anomalies*, furthering the Puritans' fascination with prodigies and portents by investigating either rare or unusual plants. But Thoreau always sought the mean or average value of nature rather than its extremes: the typical rather than the particular or unusual, the statistical rather than the anecdotal. Instead of studying the sort of windblown outliers that might have reached Concord from the prairies of Indiana or Illinois, he devoted himself to seeds that, in Nabhan's words, landed "no more than a couple hundred yards from their mother plants." Thoreau pointedly admits, "I omit the unusual—the hurricanes and earthquakes—and describe the common."

The true wonder of the statistical mean or average was that it seemed to reveal something hidden *within* the data—a kind of transcendental reality, so to speak. An early journal entry reads, "The golden mean, in ethics as in physics, is the centre of the system, and that about which all revolve; and though, to a distant and plodding planet, it is the uttermost extreme, yet, when that planet's year is complete, it will be found central." After his survey of Walden Pond disclosed that "the line of greatest length intersected the line of greatest breadth *exactly* at the point of greatest depth," Thoreau essentially turned the interval between his inner and outer life into a transcendental form of geometry. "What I have observed of the pond is no less true in ethics," he exclaims. "It is the law of average. Such a rule of the two diameters not only guides us toward the sun in the system and the heart of man, but draws lines through the length and breadth of the aggregate of a man's particular daily behaviors and waves of life into his coves and inlets, and where they intersect will be the height or depth of his character."

The same kind of thinking framed the observations and measurements Thoreau made on each of his daily walks. He always looked for the aggregate, the law of average, which might emerge from the data he'd experienced and compiled over a period of many years. An essay like "Autumn Tints"—where Thoreau carefully outlines the sequence in which autumn showed its true colors in Concord, beginning with the purple grasses and ending with the scarlet oak—was a perfect example of nature's mean. Though he complained that "the most natural system is still so artificial," Thoreau came to believe that if data were systematically collected and evaluated, nature's *own* system would reveal itself.

That's why he eventually began a project he called the Kalendar, which was basically a sequence of monthly charts or graphs, each divided into a series of rows and columns like a modern spreadsheet. In the rows running down the left-hand column he listed a number of natural phenomena; across the top of the other columns he enumerated the years. As we might expect from someone hoping to create a new calendar, the basic phenomena he singled out could be a bit quirky and oddly divided. Going down the rows for the month of November, for example, we see such items as "River Lowest," "River Highest," "Rain in First half," "Rain in last half," "NE storm," "Thunder & lightning," "Rainbow," "Foul in *AM*, pleasant in *Pm*," "1st really cold & wintry weather." Yet as unconventional as these data points may seem at times, Thoreau plainly believed that by collecting them in a systematic, coherent manner, they would somehow reveal nature's transcendental mean. Sadly, he died before proving or disproving his hypothesis—leaving us with little more than a tantalizing hint of what the poem to be called Concord might have looked like if he'd finished it.

———

Thoreau's mania for the law of average is a reminder that Concord was a singularly benign landscape during his lifetime: a kind of environmental golden mean very rare for those days. Few areas of the country were as settled as eastern Massachusetts, which was as pastoral then as it is woodsy today, having been divided into an irregular medley of rolling fields and lush meadows occasionally interrupted by woodlots and waste areas. There were no major floods or droughts in the region, no catastrophic crop failures, no devouring clouds of locusts or grasshoppers, no devastating tree blights. Nor was there anything to fear from the Indians who had long since ceased to be hostile or even live in the area—their former presence indicated by little more than the arrowheads Thoreau had a knack for finding.

The same thing was true of most other dangers great and small. Lacking the forests they needed for protection, the major predators of the region—cougars, wolves, and bears—had either been hunted to extinction or migrated away. In fact, large, undomesticated animals of any sort were so rare that when a deer wandered into a nearby town, the local paper treated it as front-page news. Since minor pests like black flies and no-see-ums relied on the same forest cover, even they weren't a problem. Imagine how shocked Thoreau would have been in San Diego, say— where Mary Austin noted that the fleas were so thick that "if you took a handful of the top soil, half of it hopped out and the rest of it ran through your fingers." Or compare Thoreau's dream of standing neck-deep in a Concord swamp for hours on end to the way slaves in northern New Jersey were often punished by being chained overnight in the mosquito-ridden swamps of the Meadowlands. If even a swampy wasteland could be considered safe, then anywhere Thoreau stood was a secure vantage point. He had the luxury of being able to observe and record the landscape without having to protect himself from it at the same time. And that made Concord a very special place to study nature.

This inherent sense of security may explain why one of the things Thoreau is best known for—his fine-grained knowledge of nature— can also appear most dated or misguided to modern eyes. Certainly, Thoreau's nostalgic account of Walden has nothing in common with anthropologist Philippe Descola's view that no matter where children are raised, they start to draw distinctions very early in life between entities "endowed with intentionality and others that are not." Descola himself is merely restating an insight of Charles Darwin's—who, along with everything else he's known for, was among the first to analyze our species' innate perception of danger. Using a lively visit to the zoo as his example,

Darwin had noticed that his children seemed to instinctively fear the larger predators, even though they'd never seen them before. "May we not suspect," he muses, "that the vague but very real fears of children, which are quite independent of prior experience, are the inherited effects of real dangers and abject superstitions during ancient savage times?"

When Darwin's and Descola's remarks are added to the history of the nation's frontier—a history of what Richard Slotkin has aptly labeled "regeneration through violence"—it's easy to see why most Americans have come to believe that nature is all about the "law of the jungle," "eat or be eaten," "fight-or-flight"—in short, "survival of the fittest." Jack London's *Call of the Wild* (1903), the story of a ranch dog returning to his lupine roots in Alaska, has sold many more copies than *White Fang* (1906), the story of a hybrid wolf gradually domesticated enough to choose a sheepdog as his mate. Jon Krakauer's *Into the Wild* (1996), the bestselling account of a man apparently *un*fit to survive the Alaskan winter, is now a syllabus favorite in many high schools and colleges. By contrast, both Thoreau's sheltered stay at Walden and the humble pond itself seem almost *contrary* to nature.

But survival of the fittest doesn't have to signify the world of "apex" predators and "trophic cascades"—or what's more generally called the ecology of fear. Darwin never used the phrase "survival of the fittest" until the fifth edition of *On the Origin of Species*, and even then he didn't restrict it to animals or predation. As many others have pointed out, Darwin was far more influenced by the logic of scarcity and famine outlined in Thomas Malthus's *An Essay on the Principle of Population* (1798) than by the "war of all against all" that Thomas Hobbes had made so much of in *Leviathan* (1651). Predatory behavior alone was of little interest to Darwin. Instead, he turned his attention to the scarcity and overpopulation that resulted from nature's periodic imbalances—a condition which extended to the sphere of plants, obviously, since they competed for available resources as fiercely as animals and contributed as much to the balance of nature.

Darwin's emphasis on nature's balance is undoubtedly why he seemed so important to Thoreau. *On the Origin of Species* didn't appear until 1859, and Thoreau didn't read it until 1860, but he had studied many of Darwin's earlier works and he clearly valued them for the light they shined on the sort of ideas he himself had been cultivating for years. Almost all of these ideas pointed to a nature defined by gradation and balance. Whether Thoreau called it the "economy of nature" or a golden mean—referring to the classical ideal of a middle between two extremes as well as the modern statistical median or mean—the nature he had in mind was a divine average, a Goldilocks zone. Certainly he viewed Concord itself as a Goldilocks zone. In his eyes, the town and its surroundings were neither too settled nor too wild, neither too arid nor too wet, neither too fallow nor too fecund. It was "just right." So, instead of being something different or contrary to nature, his beloved Concord was really *an ideal version* of what nature ought to be. Only the character of this ideal changed over time.

In the beginning, Thoreau pictured nature as a kind of ideal *pattern* or *form*. We can trace this belief pretty directly to a theory Goethe had developed in *The Metamorphosis of Plants* (1790) and later mentioned in his *Italian Journey* (not published until 1816, but based on diaries written during travels taking place in 1786–88). Though it isn't clear if Thoreau read the more scientific study, several of the early journal entries indicate that he admired the literary *Journey*. Among other things, he was very taken by the way it combined form and content, noting that Goethe's "object is faithfully to describe what he sees, and that, too, for the most part, in the order in which he saw it." But the part that seems to have hit him with the force of Goethe's own insight was a passage that was both lush and transcendental: "While walking in the Public Gardens of Palermo," Goethe writes, "it came to me in a flash that in the organ of the plant which we are accustomed to call the *leaf* lies the true Proteus who can hide or reveal himself in all vegetal forms. From first to last, the plant is nothing but leaf."

Thoreau embraced this botanical archetype with the zeal of any acolyte or convert. But, like the rest of his oscillating domain, it always had two sides—one animate, the other inanimate. Take the rather winsome idea of "crystalline botany" that occurred to Thoreau after noticing how the nearby trees and shrubs were covered by a "dense ice foliage" in winter. "It struck me," he remarks in the essay "Natural History of Massachusetts," "that these ghost leaves and the green ones whose forms they assume, were the creatures of but one law; that in obedience to the same law the vegetable juices swell gradually into the perfect leaf, on the one hand, and the crystalline particles troop to their standard in the same order, on the other." He says something very similar in an early, undated journal entry, noting, "some one has said he could write an epic to be called the leaf—and this would seem to have been the theme of the creator himself. The leaf either plain or variegated—fresh or decayed—fluid or crystalline—is natures [*sic*] constant cipher." Years later he discovered the same homology between animate and inanimate nature in the Deep Cut above Walden Pond, referring to the thawing sands as "a truly grotesque vegetation," a "sort of architectural foliage more ancient and typical than acanthus, chicory, ivy, vine, or any vegetable leaves"; still later, he found it in the deeply scalloped shape of a scarlet oak leaf, where "the eye rests with equal delight on what is not leaf and what is leaf."

Of course, none of this prevented Thoreau from being as sensitive to the shifts in botanical science as he was to the sagging banks of the Deep Cut or the changing color of autumn leaves. He was particularly attuned to the ins-and-outs of British botany, and as historian Philip Rehbock has shown, British botanists were growing more and more skeptical of a paradigm known as "final causation" in which nature was assumed to represent God's purpose and plan. Instead, they were turning to a kind of hybrid or half-hearted notion of "efficient causation"—more commonly referred to as "the distribution of organized beings in space and time"—that would eventually lead to Darwin's lucid theory of gradation, imbalance, and natural selection. Though only Darwin himself may have glimpsed what lay ahead, virtually everyone at the time understood what had to be left behind.

I can't say that Thoreau ever renounced Goethe's leafy archetype altogether. But he clearly found fellowship with the various botanists and geologists he was reading. Only someone exposed to their dynamic view of nature could have associated the formal properties of a leaf with the "sandy overflow" of a railroad embankment. And yet Thoreau's belief in a golden mean meant that he almost always focused on the way nature sought to restore any imbalances that arose, and he seemed to feel that nature was somehow less itself when they lingered. "I was struck by the orderly arrangement of trees, as if each knew its own place," he wrote near the end of his life. "As if in the natural state of things, when sufficient time is given, trees will be found occupying the places most suitable to each, but when they are interfered with, some are prompted

to grow where they do not belong and a certain degree of conf[
produced. That is, our forest generally is in a transition state to [
and normal condition."

The very idea of a normal condition implied that nature changed in order to stay about the same. Even *as* it changed, there were no severe fluctuations or losses—nothing like the "punctuated equilibrium" that paleontologists Niles Eldridge and Stephen Jay Gould would propose more than a century later, nothing like the thousands of eggs a fish might produce to guarantee the survival of a few hundred—merely the slow gradations that made Thoreau so happy. "There is no French Revolution in Nature, no excess," he writes in the journal. "She is warmer or colder by a degree or two." Another journal entry, also written late in life, epitomizes the sort of homeostatic development or "transition state" Thoreau had in mind: "By a beautiful law of distribution, one creature does not too much interfere with another. I do not hear the song sparrow here. As the pines generally increase, and a wood-lot is formed, these birds will withdraw to new pastures, and the thrushes, etc., will take their place."

Thoreau was especially interested in the dispersion of seeds—and not just in the *fact* of dispersion but in the way seeds amplified their dispersion by skittering across the frozen surfaces of ponds and traveling in the guts of animals. Indeed, the longer he thought about it, the more Thoreau concluded that seeds were the principal agent of distribution in nature, a relatively new insight at the time. However, he also saw seeds as the principal agent of gradation and stability—a *seasonally regulated* distribution favoring the orderly arrangement of nature. Seeds carried the seasons within themselves: they expressed the orderly novelty of lapsed time, the gradual transition that preserved the golden mean from one year to the next; they showed that nature never reached a "culminating point," that it always renewed itself within a narrow range. A fallen tree merely made room for the sapling at its feet.

Naturally, Thoreau wouldn't be Thoreau if he didn't choose to speak for the uniformity of nature by making the most of its intervals or edges. That's another reason his favorite seasons of the year were spring and fall—the periods of greatest change. His journal entries tend to expand during these periods, growing denser with detail and emotion, as if he had to slow nature's accelerating variety to see it whole. He began to break the seasons themselves into smaller and smaller intervals of time—speaking of "snake summer or snakes' week" and "the season of morning frogs"—because he believed "the year has many seasons more than are recognized in the almanac." Likewise, he began to segment his circle of ten miles' radius into smaller and smaller intervals of space— naming them Painted-Cup Meadow, or Grape Cliff, or Cardinal Ditch. But his most significant intervals of all were the Concord swamps. Over and over again in his walks and writings Thoreau returns to the nearby swamps—Hubbard's Swamp, Gowing's Swamp, Kibbe Place Swamp— referring to them in the essay "Walking" as "a sacred place—a *sanctum sanctorum.*"

What makes this choice so interesting is that swamps were usually thought to be the same through and through. In fact, they were often equated with deserts because people took them to be so uniform—as over-grown, dense, and dark as deserts were open, flat, and empty. Read almost any New England captivity narrative and you'll find that the landscape the narrator describes isn't just frightening but featureless—one swampy or wooded encampment after another, each exactly like the last, each as forgettable as the last. Leave it to Thoreau, then, to turn this ostensibly barren uniformity on its head, using his own view of swamps to transform Concord into the sort of interrelated network of plants and animals that we now think of as a bioregion. Philippe Descola would say that Thoreau effectively redefined the "ontological properties" of both the "swamp" and "nature," making room for a new relationship between them.

Late in 1856, in a journal entry where he recalls that he had begun to study botany by learning the popular names and localities of plants "without any regard to the plant" itself, Thoreau singles out his desire to know more about swamps as the reason he had gradually developed a more detailed and systematic approach to nature as a whole.

> I remember gazing with interest at the swamps about those days and won-dering if I could ever attain to such familiarity with plants that I should know the species of every twig and leaf in them, that I should be acquainted with every plant (excepting grasses and cryptogamous ones), summer and winter, that I saw. Though I knew most of the flowers, and there were not in any particular swamp more than half a dozen shrubs that I did not know, yet these made it seem like a maze to me, of a thousand strange species,

and I even thought of commencing at one end and looking it faithfully and laboriously through till I knew it all.

This was a remarkable piece of writing at the time, for Thoreau plainly saw the local swamps as a rich and complex environment rather than a desert or wasteland. He understood that the enveloping density of a swamp should be a measure of its diversity, not its uniformity. To say this diversity was like a maze was only to admit that he didn't know the swamp well enough at first to distinguish its differences, its internal edges and boundaries, its subtle balance of plant and animal life. Much of the swamp was actually hidden from him then, veiled by its deceptively still waters, its thick tussocks and branches. How was he to know the bottom was teeming with muskrats, mud turtles, and large pouts (a kind of fish) until he took the time to look? How was he to know that Gowing's Swamp in particular was divided into three parts—"first, the thin woody; second, the coarse bushy or gray; and third, the fine bushy or brown"?

But if Thoreau started with nothing more than a desire to identify the different species of a swamp, he gradually realized they were part of a much larger unit in which the meaning or effect of any single species might change from one season to the next. The actual name of a species turned out to be far less important than where it was located and how it evolved, and what began as a simple vocabulary lesson became a far more complex and rule-driven lesson in grammar. Once Thoreau learned the rudiments of this grammar, he was able to turn the maze "of a thousand strange species" into an orderly, if still partial, view of an environment slowly developing over time.

From there, he began to understand how a swamp itself developed. After an even closer study of Gowing's Swamp, for example, Thoreau found that in addition to being divided into three parts horizontally, from west to east, it was also divided into three parts vertically, from top to bottom.

> The filling up of a swamp, then, in this case at least, is not the result of a deposition of vegetable matter washed into it, settling to the bottom and leaving the surface clear, so filling it up from the bottom to the top; but the vegetation first extends itself over it as a film, which gradually thickens till it supports shrubs and completely conceals the water, and the under part of this crust drops to the bottom, so that it is filled up first at the top and the bottom, and the middle part is the last to be reclaimed from the water.

Herbert Wendell Gleason, *Northwest cove of Walden, ice breaking up (train in distance), March 31, 1920.* Courtesy of Concord Free Public Library.

Though brief, this, too, is a beautifully rendered account: measured, meticulous, based on prolonged observation and thought. Nor would it be Thoreau's final account of Gowing's Swamp. He would keep filling up the watery gaps in his knowledge the way the swamp itself was filling up. At one point, unable to resist the instincts of a surveyor, he paced it in two directions and produced a sketchy map to go along with his verbal descriptions. Both as literature and as science, Thoreau's ongoing study of Gowing's Swamp is as good an illustration as any of a "total object, complete with missing parts" that Samuel Beckett found so intriguing.

Thoreau truly came into his own when he began to understand the swamp not just as a *diverse* environment but as an *interdependent*

Dennis Oppenheim, *Accumulation Cut*, 1968. 100-foot trench cut perpendicular to waterfall. Gasoline powered chain saw. 24 hours required to refreeze. Frozen Bebe Lake, Ithaca, New York. Courtesy of Dennis Oppenheim Estate.

one—where plants and animals relied on each other for their existence. At first his view was fairly simple: bees pollinate flowers, mud turtles eat pouts, frogs lay their eggs in protective reeds, and pollywogs become bird food when the swamp becomes shallower and shrinks in summer. But as he began to pay attention to the way plants and animals slowly spread or disappeared, he also began to think of nature as an intricate, finely spun web of plant and animal life. Thoreau wasn't just suggesting how to make a picture when he said, "the red squirrel should be drawn with a pine cone." He was clarifying that seeds close to pine trees provided food for red squirrels and that after eating them red squirrels helped to scatter these seeds to areas where new trees had room to grow. Pine cones and squirrels were two aspects of the same object—a gestalt. When one of these aspects was altered or destroyed, so was the object as a whole. "He who cuts down woods beyond a certain limit exterminates birds."

Yet Thoreau was interested in something even more complex than how plants and animals helped each other to survive. He was also interested in how they lived together harmoniously—exemplifying the evolving equipoise of natural forces. He began with the small-scale harmonies of squirrel and cone, and then spiraled outward to larger and more complex phenomena. One of my favorite examples is his lovely analysis of the relationship between domesticated cows and wild apple trees. Tracing the life of a single tree, Thoreau observed that when it first sprang up as a small bush, the cows quickly browsed the bush to such a paltry nub that it appeared to have little chance of survival. Over the years, though, "putting forth two short twigs for every one cut off," the small "twiggy mass" became "as solid and impenetrable as a rock." This allowed the tender inner branches of the bush to grow and expand, until at last they were so broad and mature "that they become their own fence" and the heart of the bush could shoot up as a tree. Eventually, the tree reached its full height, its bushy bottom disappeared, and it generously permitted "the now harmless cows to come in and stand in its shade." The tree even allowed the cows to eat some of its fruit, "and so disperse the seed." Thus, Thoreau discovered that the cows leisurely created "their own shade and food," while the tree, no longer a bush, lived "a second life, as it were."

This and many other fine examples show how Thoreau inflated the single interval of Gowing's Swamp into a more universal view of nature. Just three sentences after saying that the variety of swamp life had convinced him to study it from one end to the other, he conscientiously expands his botanical horizon to encompass the entire poem he called Concord.

I soon found myself observing when plants first blossomed and leafed, and I followed it up early and late, far and near, several years in succession, running to different sides of the town and into the neighboring towns, often between twenty and thirty miles in a day. I often visited a particular plant four or five miles distant, half a dozen times within a fortnight, that I might know exactly when it opened, beside attending to great many others in different directions and some of them equally distant, at the same time. At the same time I had an eye for birds and whatever else might offer.

Obviously, Thoreau wasn't fully awake yet to the intricate relationship between plants and animals. They seemed to coexist, live side by side in the same vicinity, rather than forming an ecological unit or bioregion. But his original interest in swamps led to a perspective in which nature was an evolving gestalt of plants and animals and the survival of the fittest was a model of stability and balance. Near the end of his life, on a cool day in May, Thoreau noticed a bird zigzagging across the bark of a tree and concluded that "the whole North American forest is being thus explored for insect food now by several hundred species of birds. Each is visited by many kinds, and thus the equilibrium of the insect and the vegetable kingdom is preserved. Perhaps I may say that each opening bud is thus visited before it has fully expanded." That he refers to the insect and vegetable kingdom in the singular, not the plural, shows just how much nature had become a single object with different aspects—an *ecological* gestalt, defined by the harmonious coevolution of plant and animal life.

It goes without saying that both science and the world have changed so profoundly since Thoreau died that even some of his most acute observations can seem as primitive to us as Anghiera's description of the possum would have seemed to him. An obvious example is the Kalendar, which he believed would reveal nature's regularities, its divine average, though it soon became apparent the globe was actually emerging from the anomaly of the Little Ice Age (1350–1850). On a smaller scale, I would point to something like the sap-sucking aphid that occasionally cropped up in his journal, including the really large one, "the father of all the aphides," he discovered on a huckleberry leaf, and the somewhat smaller one he saw floating down the Assabet River on a maple leaf. Because of biologists like Edward O. Wilson, we now know that certain plants secrete an "airborne vapor" that suppresses the sap-sucking aphid, stimulates neighboring plants to secrete their own "defensive chemicals," and attracts a species of small wasp able to "parasitize aphids." Even if Thoreau had wanted to, he wouldn't have been able to detect this or countless other examples of coevolution. At best, he might have noticed that small wasps seemed to be present when there were a lot of aphids. But the underlying grammar of these phenomena would have been invisible to him because he lacked the instruments to measure them.

Nor could Thoreau have known just how *much* life there was around him. He often reveled in the visible signs of nature's extravagance—noting in the journal, for instance, "I have been surprised to discover the amount and the various kinds of life which a single shallow swamp will sustain." But if Linnaeus completed his binomial system believing there were about twenty thousand species in the world, we have since discovered there are at least two million—with the *actual* number, as Wilson informs us, "not known even to the nearest order of magnitude." Obviously, ours is an exponentially richer world than even Thoreau imagined, at least in part because so many of these species are too small to be seen by the naked eye or only found in obscure habitats. How could he have recognized, as we do, that the vast majority of animal phyla live on the ocean floor or that nematode worms make up four out of every five animals on earth? How could he have foreseen a world in which sixty-nine thousand species of fungi have been identified and named, with scientists projecting an additional 1.5 million still to be identified? After all, even our own accumulated knowledge can look measly or dated from one decade to the next. Before 1988, scientists had no idea that bacteria of the genus *Prochlorococcus* are probably the most abundant organisms on earth. It was the biological equivalent of discovering that the universe is mostly made up of dark matter.

Add genetics to the mix, and Thoreau's writings can seem especially dated. Even now it's hard to believe that a forest of quaking aspen in Utah is actually the clone of a single tree, or that the same thing is true of an inconspicuous circle of creosote bushes in the Mojave Desert and the waving prairies of seagrass off the island of Ibiza. Still, the differences go much deeper than this. Geneticists like Craig Venter are so taken with Erwin Schrödinger's idea of "code-script" that they've been trying to re-cast the entire field of biology as an information science. And they're not just indulging in a new metaphor, like comparing the human heart to a pump or the brain to a computer. Among other things, DNA "bar codes" are now used to distinguish one species from another—and, even more interesting, nonbiological information can be stored by certain kinds of DNA. According to the evolutionary biologist Richard Dawkins, whenever we think of seed dispersal these days we should picture millions and millions of plants around the world showering down code-script. Indeed, as Dawkins puts it, "it couldn't be any plainer if it were raining floppy discs." Things have become so advanced that we now need to make a distinction between real life (the analog, everyday world of Thoreau's writings), artificial life (the digital world of computers and algorithms), and synthetic life (the digital world of biology)—with the synthetic version defined by Venter as "self-replicating biology based on a synthetic genome, a synthetic code-script." While Thoreau thought of life as inherently literal or real, we've begun to think of it as anything logically possible to manufacture.

Many years ago, Jorge Luis Borges imagined a code-script world in "The Library of Babel," a story in which "all the books, no matter how diverse they might be, are made up of the same elements" and "it suffices that a book be possible for it to exist." In the past decade or two a new generation of artists and writers have begun to explore the possibilities of code-script by actually manipulating DNA. Among the most intriguing examples I've come across is poet Christian Bök's *Xenotext Experiment* (begun 2002). In a manifesto of the same name, Bök explains how he hopes to create a new form of poetry by implanting a synthetic genetic sequence into the bacterium *Deinococcus radiodurans*: "I plan to compose my own text in such a way that, when translated into a gene and then integrated into the cell, the text nevertheless gets 'expressed' by the organism, which, in response to this grafted, genetic sequence, begins to manufacture a viable, benign protein—a protein that, according to the original, chemical alphabet, is itself another text."

These works of Borges and Bök may suggest why some of Thoreau's more idealist notions have held up better than some of his botany. In fact, his intuitions were extremely solid, even though his science was limited by the largely pre-Darwinian era he lived in. One example is the classical notion of a golden mean—the law of averages, the middle between two extremes—that Thoreau made so much of. It turns out that genes that survive over long periods of time are very good at living in what Dawkins calls "the average environment of the species." Aside from carrying traits that modestly improve the species—slightly raising the average ability of a plant, say, to subdue aphids or attract small wasps—such genes survive because they add to an average environment that benefits all the other genes they're likely to share a body with. Evidently every species is in some sense the biological expression of a divine average.

A more curious example is Thoreau's notion of crystalline botany. On its face this "foliate structure," as he called it, might seem little more than a poetic fancy, especially since it combined animate and inanimate nature. But if Venter is any judge, modern genetics had a similar beginning—epitomized by a paper Schrödinger published in 1944 called "What is Life?" Best known for his work in quantum mechanics, Schrödinger addressed the problem of heredity by reasoning that life had to obey the laws of physics too. He suggested that chromosomes needed to contain "an elaborate code-script" and that the code-script itself needed to contain "a well-ordered association of atoms, endowed with sufficient resistivity to keep its order permanently." He called this well-ordered state an "aperiodic crystal," using the term "crystal" to signify structure and stability, and "aperiodic" to mean that it carried a lot of information. This turned out to be a crucial insight—one of the most crucial in the history of biology, according to Venter. After codiscovering the structure of DNA with James Watson, Francis Crick wrote Schrödinger to say that "your term 'aperiodic crystal' is going to be a very apt one."

Strangest of all, perhaps, is the way the supposedly parochial landscape of Concord can now be seen. Consider Wilson's observation that one of the most noteworthy traits of human beings is where we choose to live. Like Thoreau, most adults are drawn to an environment that resembles that of their childhood. But in 1994 the conceptual artists Vitaly Komar and Alex Melamid asked a random sampling of people from the United States and Russia to describe the perfect landscape painting. Much to their surprise, they found that, regardless of where people lived, they preferred an open, expansive landscape that included a secure vantage point, several groves of trees, some form of water, and a scattering of both humans and domesticated animals. Several other cross-cultural studies comparing attitudes in Europe, North America, Korea, and Nigeria corroborated this finding, and most evolutionary biologists now believe that we instinctively select for a landscape that either resembles or derives from the savannas and transitional forests where humanity arose. Evidently, we still hark back to what Wilson labels "a secure position framed by the semienclosure of a domicile." Examples of this sort of landscape can be found throughout history. Ancient Hebrews called it Canaan; Romans called it the Campania; English aristocrats called it a private estate designed by Humphry Repton or "Capability" Brown; and Thoreau—surrounded by Poplar Hill, the Great Meadow, Merrick's Pasture, Stow's Woods, Emerson's apple orchard, Walden Pond, and the sound of the local militia practicing—called it Concord. Accidentally or not, his personal ideal was also a human ideal.

I mention these things to suggest that Thoreau's writings are likely to remain relevant in ways we still can't predict. They're *inherently* "cimeter"-like, double-edged, dynamic—their "sweet edge" dividing us "through the heart and marrow" with the force of any clearly described fact. What if we were to say, for instance, that a belief in the homeostatic harmony of nature was among Thoreau's greatest weaknesses? Whether he derived this belief from the pastoral state of Concord, a version of Goethe's botanical model, or some combination of the two, it definitely owes more to Plato than Darwin. Yet it's also one of Thoreau's greatest strengths—the very thing that awakened him to what we now think of as an ecological imagination. Maybe he started out believing that all he had to do was learn the name of every plant and animal in a Concord swamp because the swamp itself remained more or less the same. But after wading through these swamps day after day, year after year, soaking up the *relation between* plants and animals as well as their genus and species, Thoreau stepped onto dry land again with a far more energetic and evolutionary view of uniformity. Now he knew something of nature's grammar, not just its vocabulary, and he was able to see its "hard bottom" as a state of constant change. "More than any other botanist of his time," Nabhan has written, "Thoreau moved past the mere naming of trees—the nouns of the forest—to track its verbs: the birds, rodents, and insects that pollinate flowers or disperse seeds, and all the other agents that shape the forest's structure."

Nature was Thoreau's milieu and his medium—indicated by his claim that "the roots of letters are things." I believe he should be taken at his word when he says, "Here I have been these forty years learning the language of these fields that I may better express myself." Separating the quality of Thoreau's art from the quality of his science never made much sense and it makes even less sense now. The double-sided quality of his work proves how much he derived his authority as a writer from an authentic understanding of nature, and plainly he would be among the first to say that better science makes for better art. When Ellery Channing famously subtitled his biography of Thoreau "The Poet-Naturalist," he gave equal weight to the two terms, knowing that the oscillation between art and science was among the most important of Thoreau's many intervals. This oscillation played out with greater and greater force as Thoreau grew older. Eventually it led to the beauty of the late natural history essays, as well as the lengthier, unfinished drafts of *Wild Fruits* and *The Dispersion of Seeds*. But all of these works were themselves shaped by what is easily Thoreau's most original contribution to both art and science: what he called "the wild."

CHAPTER 6

Wildness

Like all the other artists credited with inventing American land art—a list that includes Walter De Maria, Michael Heizer, Nancy Holt, Dennis Oppenheim, and Robert Morris—Robert Smithson was eager to move beyond the aesthetic confines of the New York gallery system. For much of the nineteenth and twentieth centuries, artworks had remained comfortably indoors, with almost every painting or sculpture meant to be seen within a space defined by neutral white walls and artificial lighting. On the whole, these works were made of metal, marble, clay, canvas, paint, paper, ink, and charcoal, with a few "found objects" thrown in for contrast and the suggestion of a grittier, more demotic world outside the world of art. Iconoclasts such as Marcel Duchamp and Robert Rauschenberg claimed to be working in the gap between art and life, but their "ready-mades" and "combines" were essentially half measures that could never be perceived as art outside the gallery or museum.

When Smithson crossed the Hudson River to explore the derelict quarries and "man-made geological networks" of New Jersey, he began to create beauty and meaning in a space which had traditionally been considered outside the sphere of art altogether—a non-space, so to speak, or what he called a "low profile," "zero panorama" space. Though he never abandoned painting and drawing, Smithson increasingly turned to dump trucks, bulldozers, and backhoes, constructing a series of works that can still seem unorthodox almost half a century later. In *Asphalt Rundown* (1969) he filled a large dump truck with blacktop and tilted it down the side of a quarry near Rome, Italy; in *Island of Broken Glass* (1970) he proposed to bury a small islet near Vancouver, British Columbia, under a layer of crystalline shards; in *Floating Island* (1970) he proposed to drag a rusty barge planted with trees around the island of Manhattan; and in *Broken Circle/Spiral Hill* (1971) he reclaimed the green-water lake of an abandoned mining site outside of Emmen, Holland. *Spiral Jetty*, created in 1970, and still Smithson's best-known work, was built by bulldozing tons of broken rocks into the Great Salt Lake.

Smithson could be very contentious at times—another "born protestant," I suppose—and as he increasingly focused on abandoned strip mines and terraced copper pits, he often found himself working at cross-purposes with the emerging environmental movement. Of the many provocative statements he made over the years, maybe the most outrageous was something he said about Niagara Falls during an interview he gave in 1973. Four years earlier, the Army Corps of Engineers had become so alarmed by the erosion of the falls that they'd reinforced a section of the riverbed with steel rods—transforming it into a product of both natural and human engineering. Smithson noted the irony of this situation in passing, but wanted to make a much broader point about the relationship between nature and culture. "Niagara looks like a giant open pit quarry," he declared. "In other words it has high walls which offend people greatly in the strip mining regions. There are defects called 'high walls' that exist in the strip mining areas and there's a desire on the part of ecologists to slope these down. The cliffs all around Niagara suggest excavation and mining, but it's just the work of nature. So there's constant confusion between man and nature."

What most offended Smithson was the "back to nature" wing of the ecology movement—those who "would rather *retreat* to scenic beauty spots than try to make a concrete dialectic between nature and people." Smithson didn't have a quarrel with the ecologists' passion or motives but with their misguided desire for renewal. Almost every form of renewal begins retrospectively. Instead of recalibrating some aspect of the present as ground zero, it usually evokes an ideal past. The implication is that the present state of the world is a distortion or betrayal of that earlier state—which actually prophesied a different future. But Smithson didn't buy this. He believed that the back-to-nature movement essentially distorted nature itself. As he said rather dismissively in another interview, "A kind of 'virgin' beauty was established in the early days of this country and most people who don't look too hard tend to see the world through postcards and calendars so that that affects their idea of what they think nature should be rather than what it is." He was even more acerbic in the interview where he said, "there is no going back to Paradise or 19th century landscape which is basically what the conservationist attitude is."

Another way of putting this is that Smithson refused to regard the American landscape as a once-and-future Eden. He believed the landscape of the 1960s and early '70s was a densely engineered gestalt shaped by the same abrasive forces that had shaped the nation all along—forces defined by the "different types of sameness" in which nature and culture had constantly displaced each other, constantly remained out of balance, and neither aspect had prevailed. One of his most seminal contributions to land art was the notion of "rising into ruin." He introduced this concept in an essay titled "A Tour of the Monuments of Passaic, New Jersey," which was published in *Artforum* in 1967. After seeing a sign that read, "YOUR HIGHWAY TAXES 21 AT WORK," Smithson mused, "That zero panorama seemed to contain *ruins in reverse,* that is—all the construction that would eventually be built. This is the opposite of the 'romantic ruin' because the buildings don't *fall* into ruin *after* they are built but rather *rise* into ruin before they are built. This anti-romantic *mise-en-scène* suggests the discredited idea of *time* and many other 'out of date' things."

Almost inevitably, the notion of rising into ruin put him at odds with industrialists as well as ecologists—with the head of one Pacific Coast lumber company lambasting the "woodsy witchdoctors of a revived ancient nature cult" who wanted to "restore our nation's environment to its disease-ridden, often hungry wilderness stage." Nor was his work any more in step with the art world's prevailing view of landscape. In a catalogue essay written for a 1976 bicentennial exhibition—*The Natural Paradise: Painting in America 1800–1950*—the eminent art historian Robert Rosenblum summarized a long tradition of art opposed to "the grim facts of a manmade civilization":

> Wherever we look in nineteenth- and twentieth-century American landscape painting, we can find, in documentary or visionary terms, that obsessive fascination with the heavenly and hellish extremes of nature. For the nineteenth century, these vistas of luxuriant paradises, magical sunsets, awesome chasms, threatening winds, and turbulent seas seemed to provide relics of a primeval past that could locate the American continent at the origins of a grand cosmic scheme. . . . For the twentieth century, this sacrosanct world of prehistoric nature moved to a more overtly metaphorical realm, providing for the generation of artists following the First World War—from O'Keefe, Tack, Dove, and Stella to Graves and Tobey—a retreat into private, pagan mythologies that sought out the mysterious secrets of

nature as eternal truths that might oppose the grim facts of a manmade civilization. . . . From Cole to Newman, these American painters have all sought a wellspring of vital forces in nature that could create a rock-bottom truth in an era when the work of man so often seemed a force of ugliness and destruction.

On its face, this summary would seem to vindicate Thoreau's solitary withdrawal to Walden Pond rather than Smithson's astringent notion of rising into ruin. But the apparent connection between withdrawal and "rock-bottom truth" can be directly traced to the way the environmental movement had mistaken Thoreau's own "hard bottom" for a return to primeval nature. I assume that's why Smithson himself took such a dim view of Thoreau's supposedly "wishy-washy transcendentalism" once he began to focus on toxic industrial sites. After all, Smithson believed the American landscape would be improved by highlighting or protecting its "pavements, holes, trenches, mounds, heaps, paths, ditches, roads, terraces, etc." as carefully as its more pristine regions.

Smithson died in 1973, killed in a private plane crash while surveying the site for a work near Amarillo, Texas. He was only thirty-five—nine years younger than Thoreau when he died. Maybe if Smithson had lived longer he would have realized that he was among Thoreau's most direct descendants. Certainly, Thoreau confronted almost every aesthetic obstacle Smithson faced, and nothing anticipated Smithson's notion of rising into ruin better than Thoreau's liberating notion of "the wild." Since both men chose to introduce their pivotal ideas by subverting the literary genre of the excursion—Thoreau in the essay "Walking," Smithson in the essay on Passaic—I'd have to say that each in his own way was thinking along the same lines.

Thoreau came of age during an era in which Americans began to realize that a landscape that had become safe enough *for* them might not be safe enough *from* them. The early colonists had routinely viewed the New World as something to be vanquished or exploited, turning a blind eye to any environmental damage that might result from their endeavor. Sermons such as "God's Promise to his Plantations," delivered in 1630, gave religious cover to this effort by citing Genesis 1:28: "Multiply, and replenish the earth, and subdue it." At the same time, everyone, pious or impious, assumed that nature was its own worst enemy, wracked year after year by the devastating effects of earthquakes and floods or the more prosaic havoc of insects and weeds. The very certainty of this repeated deterioration implied that nature had to be vigilantly combated by husbandry and improvement.

By 1823, however, when James Fenimore Cooper's novel *The Pioneers* was published, Americans seemed to be feeling a new and different anxiety about nature. One of the novel's most exciting set pieces is a deadly, engulfing forest fire that suddenly ignites a canister of gunpowder—creating an escalating inferno that appears to be the result of human error. Cooper also includes a despairing commentary on the damage done by silver mining, a chapter on how rapaciously the forest was being cleared for potash and lumber, another on the wanton slaughter of pigeons, still another on the profligate taking of fish, and a carefully delivered warning from Leatherstocking to "use, but don't waste." While Cooper's remained a relatively solitary voice for a while, this was the moment when Americans began to see themselves as a source of environmental harm as well as husbandry. John Winthrop had warily defined the Massachusetts Bay Colony as a "community of perills," endlessly endangered by any weakness the colonists might display in their compact with each other and with God. Now the nation seemed to be imperiled by a misguided compact with nature as well. Thoreau constantly fretted that the pristine woods of Maine were being floated down the Allagash to build the wagons and houses of Massachusetts, while the painter Thomas Cole complained just as bitterly that the woods of upstate New York were being herded down the Hudson to construct the houses and factories of New York City.

On the other hand, Rosenblum's essay is just one of many indications that this was also the moment when Americans began to beatify the virgin beauty that Smithson later criticized—often associating it with what he called a "Mickey Mouse" version of Eden. In the first coffee-table book devoted to the subject—a two-volume work titled *American Scenery; or, Land, Lake, and River, Illustrations of Transatlantic Nature* (1840)—the critic Nathaniel P. Willis helped to advance an essentially nostalgic view of the nation's future. "It strikes the European traveller, at the first burst of the scenery of America on his eye," Willis wrote, "that the New World of Columbus is also a new world from the hand of the Creator"—"so vast and powerful, that he may well imagine it an Eden newly sprung from the ocean."

Though Cole was more apprehensive than Willis about the nation's future, pointing to "the iron tramp" of "meager utilitarianism," he agreed with his compatriot that "we are still in Eden" and that "the most distinctive, and perhaps the most impressive, characteristic of American scenery is its wildness." Naturally, he waxed ecstatic about Niagara Falls, referring to it as "that wonder of the world!—where the sublime and beautiful are bound together in an indissoluble chain." But in both his art and his writing he paid far more attention to the kind of scenery he found in the Catskills and the Adirondacks—a landscape whose "primitive" and picturesque nature, he believed, was the least "European" element of the rising new nation. Clearly, many Europeans themselves felt the same way, with the romantic writer François-René de Chateaubriand, for one, concluding that "her wilderness will be her way of life."

That Thoreau's view of wildness contradicted Willis's, and Cole's, and almost everyone else's at the time, is one of the reasons I believe he was both original and ahead of his time. What makes him even more unusual, however, is that he was so *far* ahead of his time—essentially a man of the twentieth and twenty-first century as well as the nineteenth. And that's mainly because he looked to the future of the nation without harking back to some ideal or imaginary past.

Concord was not just a benign landscape, after all. Pieced by its orderly fences, fields, and woodlots, it was also a *mixed* or *negotiated* landscape—a humble, zero-panorama gestalt of nature and culture. Yes, Thoreau believed "the most alive is the wildest. Not yet subdued to man." But as I noted earlier, he was quick to admit that it was "vain to dream of a wildness distant from ourselves": "It is the bog in our brain and bowels, the primitive vigor of Nature in us, that inspires that dream. I shall never find in the wilds of Labrador any greater wildness than in some recess in Concord, i.e., that I import into it." Though Emerson probably thought wildness was a rhetorical trick—yet another example of Thoreau "substituting for the obvious word and thought its diametrical opposite"— nothing could be further from the truth. In fact, it's one of the first indications of how we might respond positively to what's now called the Anthropocene, an often derogatory term referring to the era in which humanity has had a significant effect on the environment.

Thoreau didn't discover the wild the way so many explorers were said to have discovered the New World or the Far West. He "imported" it—that is, *invented* it—by standing neck-deep in the bogs and wastelands of the region and seeking out the rough, marginal, leftover strips of land that his neighboring farmers either neglected or were unable to plough. The wild was a way of seeing, an aesthetic, a language—and ultimately it signified an alternative space, so to speak, *within* Concord rather than somewhere outside or beyond it. Trafficking in the grammar of the wild encouraged Thoreau to come down from the distant mountains, to abandon the sort of sublime prospects that had made his early essays so derivative, in order to explore the ground at his feet. His very last journal entry describes the gravel patterns he encountered along the Fitchburg Railroad causeway one morning after a violent storm. Either bending close or on hands and knees, he noticed that "behind each little pebble, as a protecting boulder, an eighth or a tenth of an inch in diameter, extends northwest a ridge of sand an inch or more, which it has protected from being washed away, while the heavy drops driven almost horizontally have washed out a furrow on each side, and on all sides are these ridges, half an inch apart and perfectly parallel." The entry ends with him saying, "All this is perfectly distinct to an observant eye, and yet could easily pass unnoticed by most."

Such a lovely picture of the way wind and water textured the gravel between railroad ties shows how squarely Thoreau located the wild in the gap between nature and culture. Facing both the "barren" sameness of wilderness and the clockwork sameness of society—a joyless state the architect Rem Koolhaas has coolly designated "the fuzzy empire of blur"—Thoreau chose to create a more eccentric and peripheral gestalt that included the Fitchburg Railroad as well as Gowing's Swamp. In *Walden*, he happily admitted how often he walked into Concord along the Fitchburg causeway, especially during the winter when the snow was so quickly cleared. He was even willing to concede that "one well-conducted institution regulates a whole country." But after observing the thawing sands and clays of the Deep Cut for several years, he also concluded, "this one hillside illustrated the principle of all the operations of Nature."

Thoreau never thought of the wild as something separate or isolated from society, or as a return to some "Eden newly sprung from the earth."

Wildness represented an original *relation* to nature, not nature in its supposedly original state. That's why he typically sought the wild in the areas where society began to break down, became marginalized, gradually rose into ruin. Just as pancreatic cells can "jump change" into liver cells, so could nature jump change into culture and vice versa. Very early on, Thoreau said, "I imagine it to be some advantage to live a primitive and frontier life, though in the midst of an outward civilization." Over the course of his life, he gradually pushed this double-sided world to an extreme. The sensibility that emerged in Thoreau's later works was exquisitely attuned to the low-profile areas of wildness that waxed and waned within Concord and within Thoreau himself—areas that, like Warhol's soup cans, invariably demanded a different way of seeing to be seen in the first place. This sensibility proved that almost *anything* can beckon us to feeling if our eyes are wide open enough. Indeed, the writer W. G. Sebald has suggested that our emotions may be most deeply felt when associated with the most insignificant things.

––––––––––

Though I could list countless descriptions of the wild in Thoreau's writings, I particularly like his account of the purple grass in "Autumnal Tints." The essay as a whole is devoted to reorienting Americans' view of autumn—which, for Thoreau, is a season, an aspect of agriculture, and a poetic subject all at once. Rather than picturing apples fattening crisp and red or grapes slowly sweetening on the vine—each an echo of John Keats's iconic "Season of mist and mellow fruitfulness" in the poem "To Autumn"—Thoreau begins *his* seasonal song of praise with a deadpan, prosaic observation: "By the twentieth of August, everywhere in woods and swamps, we are reminded of the fall, both by the richly spotted Sarsaparilla-leaves and Brakes, and the withering and blackened Skunk-Cabbage and Hellebore." But even this, it turns out, is just a way of introducing the lowly, still more pedestrian "Purple Grass (*Eragrostis pectinacea*)." As Thoreau is eager to tell us, the purple grass is usually found "on waste strips or selvages of land at the base of dry hills, just above the edge of the meadows, where the greedy mower does not deign to swing his scythe; for this is a thin and poor grass, beneath his notice."

Thoreau admits that he had to discover the purple grass for himself—had to become possessed by it—before he could appreciate its beauty and wildness. Wittgenstein might describe this switch as the difference between a report and an exclamation, that is, between saying "I see the purple grass" and saying "I see the purple grass!" In any case, Thoreau's wonderfully precise description begins as a distant landscape view, dollies in like a movie camera for a close-up lesson in botany, and then pulls back again, creating a kind of *anti*-landscape in which we begin to appreciate the beauty and wildness of what we're looking at because we now know what it is and are able to see it at two different scales simultaneously.

> Standing on a hill-side near our river, I saw, thirty or forty rods off, a stripe of purple half a dozen rods long, under the edge of a wood, where the ground sloped toward a meadow. It was as high-colored and interesting, though not quite so bright, as the patches of Rhexia, being a darker purple, like a berry's stain laid on close and thick. On going to and examining it, I found it to be a kind of grass in bloom, hardly a foot high, with but few green blades, and a fine spreading panicle of purple flowers, a shallow, purplish mist trembling around me. Close at hand it appeared but a dull purple, and made little impression on the eye; it was even difficult to detect; and if you plucked a single plant, you were surprised to find how thin it was, and how little color it had. But viewed at a distance in a favorable light, it was of a fine lively purple, flower-like, enriching the earth. Such puny causes combine to produce these decided effects.

Obviously *no* such "puny causes" of beauty and wildness were likely to be cherished by Cooper, Cole, or Willis. The "greedy mower" wasn't the only one to consider such a landscape "beneath his notice." So did virtually every artist and writer of the time. To even suggest that wildness might exist at the edge of a ploughed field or the base of a stone wall was considered something more than mere ignorance or bad taste: it signified a basic misunderstanding of both nature's and society's ontological properties. How could the civilized and the wild exist within the same conceptual space? How could someone in an urbane, mercantile town like Concord just step out the door and find himself in the wild? Why would someone *want* to step out the door and find himself there? Embodied in Thoreau's account of the purple grass was a simple yet radical idea: Don't define the wild by some ideal or illusory version of nature but by its everyday features and laws.

When Thoreau decided to learn the species of every twig and leaf in Gowing's Swamp, he began to conjure up, began to *create*, the wild.

Swamps existed on the margins of society—scattered bogs surrounded by cultivated fields—and like the Deep Cut, they illustrated all of nature's laws and operations if properly understood. But because they were both an ecology unto themselves and part of a larger bioregion, swamps couldn't be properly understood unless they were viewed as marginal elements to begin with. Wildness represented an *interval between* nature and society, a gestalt, a dialectic, not a one-sided retreat or escape, much less the sort of purely aesthetic experience that had Cole rhapsodizing about "the sublime melting into the beautiful, the savage tempered by the magnificent." Wildness was Thoreau's way of saying that nature worked its wonders wherever it existed. And by casting a more empirical eye on such things as swamps and grasses, or the way cows and apple trees coevolved, he created a sphere that had never existed before.

Thoreau also thought of wildness as an extreme form of *acquaintance*. He wanted to become so familiar with the plants and animals he encountered that he would know all their names and how each and every one was related. That's why the wild was inherently an aspect of home rather than the distant woods of Labrador or Maine. John Muir later said, "The clearest way into the Universe is through a forest wilderness." But Thoreau's way into the universe, his sense of wildness, was far more intimate—the result of a close and systematic study of Concord. Remember the journal entry where he observes, "If I should travel to the prairies, I should less understand them, and my past life would serve me ill to describe them. Many a weed here stands for more of life to me than the big trees of California would if I should go there." In fact, around the time he wrote "Autumnal Tints," Thoreau was happy to associate wildness with the lumps of coal he used to heat his home. "I am interested in each contemporary plant in my vicinity, and have attained to a certain acquaintance with the larger ones. They are cohabitants with me of this part of the planet, and they bear familiar names. Yet how essentially wild they are! as wild, really, as those strange fossil plants whose impressions I see on my coal."

Ask yourself, what other artist or writer before Smithson picked up an ordinary lump of coal and saw such a liberating form of wildness? Smithson was as influenced by the quarries he visited while growing up in Passaic, New Jersey, as Thoreau was by his childhood trip to the relatively denuded shores of Walden Pond. Both made the memories of these chance outings the bedrock of their art. Toward the end of Smithson's life, as he began to associate the steeply machined walls of a strip mine with the naturally engineered gorge of Niagara Falls, he actually called himself "a geologic agent."

Of course, coal never played the kind of role in Thoreau's work that it did in, say, Smithson's controversial reclamation projects. Thoreau barely mentioned an old coal pit he stumbled into one day while surveying a neighbor's property line. But as a product of vegetation that has been slowly carbonized, even fossilized, coal can definitely be associated with Thoreau's version of rising into ruin. One of the reasons Thoreau spent so much time studying swamps was that he believed society would only advance by falling into a state of at least partial decay. "The civilized nations—Greece, Rome, England—have been sustained by the primitive forests which anciently rotted where they stand," he remarks in "Walking." "They survive as long as the soil is not exhausted." Not surprisingly, Thoreau ends his description of the sunken, crumbling old coal pit by noting that it had become a "wild, rank, luxuriant place," where "mosses and lichens abound."

Decay became one of Thoreau's greatest preoccupations. He believed that nature needed to be preserved, either intact or on the various edges of society, so that it could keep on rotting: "I would not have every man nor every part of a man cultivated, any more than I would have every acre of earth cultivated: part will be tillage, but the greater part will be meadow and forest, not only serving an immediate use, but preparing a mould against a distant future, by the annual decay of the vegetation which it supports." As he says in "Autumnal Tints," "the great harvest of the year" is not fruit or grain, but the addition of "a leaf's thickness to the depth of the soil"; it is "the beautiful way in which Nature gets her muck." Over the course of many harvests, indeed centuries of harvests, the falling leaves of autumn continue to "live in the soil, whose fertility and bulk they increase." They "stoop to rise, to mount higher in coming years, by subtle chemistry."

Admittedly, Smithson took a divergent view of rising into ruin, identifying it with the principle of entropy specified in the Second Law of Thermodynamics. Everywhere Smithson looked, he found a landscape escalating into chaos and "different types of sameness." He often spoke of "interchangeable distances" and "unfinished cities of organized

Herbert Wendell Gleason, *Old stump and woodpecker's hole, Corner Spring Woods, October 25, 1899.* Courtesy of Concord Free Public Library.

wreckage," and he insisted that nature was giving way to "incalculable cycles of nonduration." "A Tour of the Monuments of Passaic, New Jersey" culminates in the "Sandbox Monument"—a "jejune experiment" in which Smithson imagines a simple sandbox divided down the middle, with black sand on one side and white sand on the other. He notes that if someone were to run around the box a few hundred times in a clockwise direction, the sands would gradually mix and everything would begin to turn grey. But his point was that reversing this process— running around the box counterclockwise—would not return the sand to its original state of being half white, half black. Instead it would lead to an even "greater degree of greyness" and entropy.

Robert Smithson, *Upside Down Tree I, Alfred, NY*, 1969. Three original 126 format
chromogenic-development transparencies. Collection of the Estate of Robert
Smithson. Courtesy of James Cohan, New York. Art © Holt-Smithson Foundation/
Licensed by VAGA, New York, N.Y.

I really admire the conceptual elegance of this thought experiment,
but like the modern notion of genius, it isn't what Thoreau had in mind.
To understand the difference, all we need to do is substitute the melting
sands of the Deep Cut for Smithson's sandbox. Where Smithson saw a
single law of inertia at work, Thoreau saw "all the operations of Nature."
In fact, instead of degenerating into chaos or sameness, the sandy gran-
ules of the Deep Cut actually obeyed "the law to which the most inert also yields" and exemplified nature's enduring sense of order. "It is
wonderful how rapidly yet perfectly the sand organizes itself as it flows,"
Thoreau exclaims, "using the best material its mass affords to form the
sharp edges of its channel."

Smithson's sandbox had no room for sharp edges. If anything, it represented the *impossibility* of sharp edges, maybe even of form itself. Still, even Smithson clearly believed artists could create an "organized wreckage" of some sort within the interval between nature and culture. His various reclamation projects were a beautiful and compelling expression of that skeptical aesthetic and they continue to inspire my still evolving view of Thoreau.

———

Lately, I've come to see Thoreau's notion of rising into ruin as a form of the "adjacent possible"—a term the systems biologist Stuart A. Kauffman coined to highlight how "we live in an emergent universe in which ceaseless unforeseeable creativity arises and surrounds us." Kauffman is just one of many biologists, ecologists, and philosophers in recent years to endorse what is essentially a dynamic, Darwinian world view. For instance, Bruno Latour similarly celebrates a universe of "the hidden, the improbable, the surprising, the counter-intuitive." But Kauffman also believes that because the current state of reality restricts our capacity to predict future organisms or events, we need to recognize the limits of human reason. This leads him to say that we should use nature's creativity as a model for reinventing "the sacred"—by which he means a secular realm of pure contingency as well as a more religious one shaped by the Judeo-Christian tradition.

I can list many examples of what Kauffman is talking about in the secular realm. Everyday evolution is the most obvious, since gene splicing has now breached the boundaries of existing plants and animals so completely that almost any life form is possible. Land art is another example, having opened up an entirely new sphere of work by seeing the possibilities that lay beyond the most singular boundary of nineteenth-century American landscape painting, the Hudson River. Thoreau himself would probably have been intrigued by what modern cartographers call "trap streets." These are essentially fake streets, or small areas of fake terrain, added to real maps as copyright protection—a digital watermark, of sorts, used to determine whether a map has been copied and sold by someone else. There's even a website called The Sky on Trap Street that takes you to various fake streets on Google Maps, switches to Street View, and then looks up at the sky in these imaginary places. Maps of this kind are a guide to the unknown as much as the known, a way of going beyond the kind of boundaries that close down the possibilities of space rather than opening them up.

Of course, Thoreau would never have been put off by the sacred or by Kauffman's desire to reinvent that, too. Not only did he believe in a higher realm, he generally sought it in the most humble places. In "The Allagash and East Branch," the last and longest of the essays he wrote about Maine, there is a marvelous passage showing how even Thoreau's most down-to-earth observations could quickly veer in a more transcendental or sacred direction. "Standing on a mountain in the midst of a lake," he writes, "where would you look for the first sign of approaching fair weather? Not into the heavens, it seems, but into the lake"—"where there was reflected upward to us through the misty air a bright blue tinge from the distant unseen sky of another latitude beyond."

Thoreau often pointed to a "latitude beyond," and it's just one indication of how interested he was in adjacent worlds. Again, the following examples are random—neither chronological nor "best-ofs"—but I think they help to reveal the range of Thoreau's thinking. Among other things, he seems to agree with Kauffman that the perception of possibility is generally indirect, lateral, a kind of awareness of something partially sensed or grasped rather than a sudden leap into the unknown.

We live on the verge of another and purer realm, from which these odors and sounds are wafted over to us. The borders of our plot are set with flowers, whose seeds were blown from more Elysian fields adjacent. They are the pot-herbs of the Gods. Some fairer fruits and sweeter fragrances wafted over to us, betray another realm's vicinity.

All nature is in an expectant attitude.

I hear beyond the range of sound,
I see beyond the verge of sight,
New earths—new skies—new seas—around.

Having by chance recorded a few disconnected thoughts and then brought them into juxtaposition, they suggest a whole new field in which it was possible to labor and to think. Thought begat thought.

My practicalness is not to be trusted to the last. To be sure, I go upon my legs for the most part, but, being hard-pushed and dogged by a superficial common sense which is bound to near objects by beaten paths, I am off the handle, as the phrase is,—I begin to be transcendental.

It is a certain faeryland where we live. You may walk out in any direction over the earth's surface, lifting your horizon, and everywhere your path, climbing the convexity of the globe, leads you between heaven and earth, not away from the light of the sun and stars and the habitations of men.

We affirm that all things are possible, but only these things [which] have been to our knowledge.

What's most notable about Thoreau's purer realm, his latitude beyond, is that he gradually came to identify its sacredness with the average or the everyday rather than the sublime or unusual. Gowing's Swamp, the raggedy edge of a smoothly ploughed field, the thin strip of land along the base of a stone wall or a rail fence—all became magical places of preservation and renewal. Gary Snyder has spoken of "a ghost wilderness" shrouding the planet, populated by the millions of seeds embedded in the mud on birds' feet, hidden in the desert sands, and carried by the winds. But Thoreau was among the first to perceive this ethereal realm of everyday ruin and renewal: "I have great faith in a seed," he says. And, elsewhere, "The very earth itself is a granary and a seminary."

Plainly, this was very different from what "going to seed" meant to most Americans at the time. Where others saw these marginal, leftover strips of land as nothing more than that, Thoreau saw them as reservoirs for both endangered species and greater diversity. He was aware that as more and more woodland turned into fields, many species of plants and animals sought the edges and wastelands of the landscape simply in order to survive. That's why he began to pay almost as much attention to Concord's walls and fences as he did to its swamps. Ecologist David R. Foster has noted how Thoreau grew to understand that most of the walls and fences followed natural intervals or "breaks" in the landscape—intervals "defined by changes in soil or topography"—and thus represented a particularly fecund and diverse area of growth. As he began to focus on the poetry and mechanics of seed dispersal, Thoreau also came to realize that if a field were left fallow for a while, or deserted altogether, the plants and animals that had been protected along its edges would begin to expand outward again and repopulate it.

So compelling was this insight that Aldo Leopold later wrote, "There are idle spots on every farm, and every highway is bordered by an idle strip as long as it is; keep cow, plow, and mower out of these idle spots, and the full native flora, plus dozens of interesting stowaways from foreign parts, could be part of the normal environment of every citizen." The British biologist Anthony Bradshaw echoes this mongrel, negotiated point of view when he remarks that the substrates in abandoned quarries and other dry pits make them superlative refuges for the sort of rare and wild plants that are "unable to withstand the competition occurring in more fertile habitats." Obviously, Smithson's controversial proposals to reclaim idle and abandoned industrial sites took this ecological thinking to a new extreme, but he was still trafficking in the lateral opportunities of wildness.

If nothing else, then, Kauffman's notion of the adjacent possible suggests that Thoreau envisioned Concord as a lateral and hybrid landscape all along: an Eden of newly sprung weeds, a paradise pieced and ploughed, an Elysian field rising into ruin. After all, perfection excluded possibility. How could there be something *more* in a pristine or perfect world? Certainly, there was no reason to *learn* anything more in such a world—to set out each morning with a particular destination in mind and a specific hypothesis to test; to compile a detailed record of these daily pilgrimages in a journal that eventually amounted to nearly two million words; to study the various phenomena of nature so closely and accurately that it led to several new theories of the way nature worked and the outline of a more intuitive and empirical Kalendar. Perfection signified a sphere so circular and absolute that curiosity would never arise.

But wildness was always the realm of *something more, something beyond*. As Peter Sloterdijk has remarked, it wasn't until people began to seek transcendence in the earthly, sublunary "horizon beyond" rather than the ethereal "heaven above" that Thomas More came up with the idea of "Utopia," an island society he deliberately located to the west, in the New World, rather than overhead in the firmament. Thoreau's latitude beyond was his way of saying YES! to the utopian qualities of the alien, the complex, the contradictory, the unexpected, the uncertain—all aspects of the "new worlds" to be seen every day within the wavering, irregular circle of ten miles' radius he called home. Whether sacred or profane, elevated or mundane, wildness was the interval of silence that enabled Thoreau to turn these new worlds into a new "world-inner-space" and a new kind of literature. Wildness enabled him to transform the borderline, down-to-earth space of Concord into a grand and double-edged state of being. It enabled him to speak for the absolute freedom of nature in the midst of civilization. Above all, it granted nature the right to speak for itself.

Yet the very originality of Thoreau's thinking forced him to persuade everyone else that the wild actually existed. And because he also wanted to show that it *ought* to exist—that there was a sacred purpose to wildness which would lead him to declare "all good things are wild and free" and "in Wildness is the preservation of the world"—he was equally dedicated to showing it was *better* than a conventional view of nature, indicative of some *higher law* that obligated people to protect wildness at any cost. And for that, Thoreau turned to beauty.

CHAPTER 7

Beauty

Thirty miles north of New York City, just past the historic towns of Tarrytown and Sleepy Hollow, there's a largely wooded area of about fifteen hundred acres known as Rockefeller State Park Preserve. Like Walden Pond, the scenery is generally modest or low profile, something that needs to be looked at over time, seasonally, to become an intriguing foreground rather than a forgettable background.

My wife and I have an annual pass to the park and we've grown accustomed to walking its hardened dirt paths nearly every weekend. Our usual route takes us through a dense mix of hardwoods reverberating with the jittery, piercing cries of blue jays and the hard tapping of woodpeckers. At various points along the route we pass a small, reed-choked marsh where peepers briefly mark the start of spring each year; a large, downed tree with several massive boulders still lodged in its exposed roots; a lovely, tilted meadow that's lime-green in summer, reddish-ochre in winter; and numerous clumps of berry bushes, their slender, red, prickly branches inscribing gentle arcs in the air. Occasionally we startle a deer or two, wary and nearly invisible against the dappled ground cover. In early spring and fall we're treated to the sight of migrating ducks and geese splashing down in a small lake ringed with Monet-like water lilies. On hot summer days we pick the oily wineberries, holding them like rubies in our palms before eating, and in the cold light of winter we struggle through snow that has smoothed the rocky outcrops into an icy, drifted version of Maya Lin's grassy *Wavefield* at Storm King Art Center, a few miles northwest of the preserve. At every turn in the landscape, we feel surrounded by beauty.

We can thank Immanuel Kant's *Critique of Judgment*—first published in 1790—for suggesting that some of our most basic ideas of beauty should derive from landscape and nature. Certainly, this wasn't true of the ancient Greeks and Romans, who more or less invented the Western tradition of aesthetics, but were chiefly in thrall to the human body. A couplet of W. H. Auden's comes to mind: "Art's subject is the human clay, / And landscape but a background to a torso." The Romans in particular—or so Alexander von Humboldt tells us— were so indifferent to sublime, mountainous landscapes that Julius Caesar once crossed the Alps without ever setting foot outside his carriage, content to complete a book of grammar instead of admiring the spectacular scenery.

Thoreau's debt to the *Critique* is apparent in the way he came to think about nature and the way he proposed to preserve it. Mainly, Kant taught Thoreau to see nature on its own terms and for its own sake. But he also taught Thoreau to see nature for what it might be as well as for what it was. And in an early form of future shock, Thoreau came to realize that the landscape he sought to invent each day, the landscape that was so endearing to *him*, was threatened by one of the very things that made it so endearing to *others*.

Nowhere is this clearer than in Thoreau's final essays on natural history, which are shadowed by an impending sense of loss and culpability. There are four of them—"Autumnal Tints," "The Succession of Forest Trees," "Wild Apples," and "Huckleberries"—and while they vary in mood and purpose, all raise a red, autumnal flag. Sometimes Thoreau is resigned and sad, as when he observes with a pomaceous sigh, "The era of the Wild Apple will soon be past. It is a fruit which will probably become extinct in New England." At other times he's almost outraged, his tone more strident, closer to that of "Slavery in Massachusetts": "What sort of country is that where the huckleberry fields are private property? When I pass such fields on the highway, my heart sinks within me. I see a blight on the land."

These and other comments suggest that Thoreau spent the final years of his life trying to stem this escalating blight by convincing the people of Concord to *take a different view of improvement*. Long before "location, location, location" became a familiar mantra, Americans were obsessed by the idea of "improvement, improvement, improvement." This was especially true of New Englanders. As Henry Adams later wrote of the "complete Virginia education" he'd received on a dreary, potholed road to Mount Vernon, "To the New England mind, roads, schools, clothes, and a clean face were connected as part of the law of order or divine system. Bad roads meant bad morals." But Thoreau wanted to stress a countervailing set of values, to indicate the outlines of a new moral universe. "All our improvements, so called, tend to convert the country into the town," he remarks in "Huckleberries." "I do not say this by way of complaining of this custom in particular, which is beginning to prevail .... It is my own way of living that I complain of as well as yours—and therefore I trust that my remarks will come home to you."

If the essays have an ironic bite at times, maybe it's because Thoreau felt that his remarks *hadn't* struck home, or not yet anyway, not like they had when he spoke out against slavery or the war against Mexico. Apparently his neighbors were more eager to hear what he had to say about John Brown than Johnny Appleseed, suggesting that it's always harder to accept a totally new idea than deal with the contradictions of an old one. Most of his neighbors felt that slavery violated the state's principles of freedom and equality, and ought to be abolished on those grounds. But what did the loss of wild apples have to do with anything? And why was Thoreau happier to see a farmer up to his neck in a swamp than out plowing his fields? Surely there wasn't any reason to consider private property and improvement *bad*!

Thoreau kept reaching out to his neighbors, kept stressing how readily the sounds of the village green carried to the shores of Walden Pond, because he hoped that his essays would ultimately persuade them to change their minds about improvement. In effect, he was addressing his remarks to what the philosopher John Dewey would later call a new public—which in this case meant an environmentally conscious public, an environmentally *sympathetic* public, alert to the various dangers associated with improvement and willing to regulate it in order to protect nature against those dangers.

Thoreau clearly came to believe that the only way to approach this public was by relying on the moral suasion of natural beauty. One of his most significant journal entries is the one from 1852 in which he says, "Nature has looked uncommonly bare and dry to me for a day or two. With our senses applied to the surrounding world we are reading our own physical and corresponding moral revolutions. Nature was so shallow all at once I did not know what had attracted me all my life. I was therefore encouraged when, going through a field this evening, I was unexpectedly struck with the beauty of an apple tree. The perception of beauty is a moral test." That beauty also became the moral test of Thoreau's new public is hardly surprising—not least because it's an essential feature of the *Critique* as well. Kant wrote the *Critique* to show that taking a close and sustained interest in natural beauty was both the sign of a good soul and favorable to moral feeling. But he also turned to beauty because he feared that morality itself would never be anything more than an abstract set of rules unless people were prepared to act upon those rules.

Of course, an uncertainty of this kind is part of any moral system trusting to choice rather than coercion, and Kant loathed almost any form of coercion. Asked to choose between Sparta or Athens, Lycurgus or Solon, he would have opted for Solon every time. Happily, a sense of beauty is both universal and singular, common to every human being but peculiar to each of us. At the same time, it's very down to earth, suggesting that morality begins with the sort of basic impressions that give us pleasure as well as knowledge of the world. If anything seems to offer a compelling yet democratic means of turning tough or intangible principles into moral sentiments and actions, it is beauty. Thus we find Thoreau noting as early as 1843 that beauty represents "a medium intellectual state" between the elementary data of empiricism and the more "enlightened moment" in which the laws of nature became "morality and modes of divine life." Thus we also find some of the most compelling passages in the essay "Autumnal Tints," devoted to what the political and cultural theorist Jane Bennett has called a "deliberately cultivated sensibility." "Objects are concealed from our view," Thoreau explains, "not so much because they are out of the course of our visual ray as because we do not bring our minds and eyes to bear on them."

> There is just as much beauty visible to us in the landscape as we are prepared to appreciate,—not a grain more. The actual objects which one man will see from a particular hill-top are just as different from those which another will see as the beholders are different. The Scarlet Oak must, in a sense, be in your eye when you go forth. We cannot see anything until we are possessed with the idea of it, take it into our heads,—and then we can hardly see anything else.

Exactly *what* Thoreau chose to see as beautiful is one of the things that makes his nature writing so noteworthy. To counter the view that beauty was mostly in the eye of the beholder, Kant had argued that calling something beautiful was always an objective appraisal—and because it *was* objective, it carried with it an expectation that others would agree with it. While this meant that beauty was an imperative, it was more in the nature of a demand than a dictate. Saying that others *ought* to agree with you didn't mean they *would*; they had to be persuaded. This was especially true if the basic idea of beauty was in question, as it was time and again during the modernist period, for instance, when almost every swerve or jump in style was accompanied by a manifesto excoriating all earlier art and celebrating the one and only art to come. Naum Gabo and Antoine Pevsner's *Realistic Manifesto* of 1920 was typical: "Space and time are re-born to us today. Space and time are the only forms on which life is built and hence art must be constructed."

Thoreau was hardly an avant-garde writer, at least not as we usually define this term. But he was equally committed to a new and unexplored world. As much as he wanted others to see and assent to the beauty of nature, he also wanted them to think of beauty itself differently. That's what his detailed description of the scarlet oak and the purple grass really amounted to. Likewise his descriptions of Walden Pond, the Deep Cut, and Gowing's Swamp. All pointed to a transfiguring new view of natural beauty, and all implied that the new environmental public he had in mind had to arise from the imperatives of a new and wilder aesthetic as well.

Like the *Critique* itself, Thoreau harked back to a Platonic notion of "appropriateness"—meaning that he considered nature most beautiful where it appeared to be most nearly an end in itself, operating according to its own laws. Singling out a maple tree, for example, Thoreau says, "It has faithfully discharged the duties of a Maple there, all winter and summer, neglected none of its economies, but added to its stature in the virtue which belongs to a Maple, by a steady growth for so many months, never having gone gadding abroad, and is nearer heaven than it was in the spring." He puts it even more succinctly in a journal entry: "It is remarkable how true each plant is to its season."

Pivoting in this direction led Thoreau to derive his notion of beauty from what amounted to an ecological and evolutionary understanding of nature, not the usual aesthetic categories. In fact, to say what he said about something as ordinary as a pincushion gall was like thumbing his nose at almost every artistic doctrine of the day: "The pincushion galls on young white oaks are now among the most beautiful objects in the

ds, coarse woolly white to appearance, spotted with bright red or
ison on the exposed side. It is remarkable that a mere gall, which at
ᴍꜱᴛ we are inclined to regard as something abnormal, should be made
so beautiful, as if it were the *flower* of the tree; that a disease, an excres-
cence, should prove, perchance, the greatest beauty,—as the tear of the
pearl."

Clearly, the world becomes a very different place if looking into the
face of nature includes the possibility of nature looking back. By seeking
an interval of some kind between the cultivated fields of Massachusetts
and the primitive forests of Maine, Thoreau began to discover the sorts
of places that most people thought of as wasted or not worth looking at
in the first place: wild areas, democratic areas, areas that were not just
marginal or ignored, but patently ugly when judged by anything other
than the standards of nature itself. That's how nature looked back—by
insisting on a new standard of beauty. Unfortunately, because these areas
were a byproduct of improvement, they were also the places that would
be lost if improvement went unchecked—which is why all of Thoreau's
late environmental writings bid the American public to modify its view
of improvement.

Thoreau understood that he couldn't just *address* a new public. Both
morally and practically, he had to *create* one. Though it's never clear just
how large this public is supposed to be—Thoreau was always vague on
such matters—its basic form seems to correspond to the kind of entity
later described by John Dewey in *The Public and Its Problems* (1927).
Dewey himself was mainly interested in the public that defined the
modern democratic state, but he believed that a public arose whenever
there was a common perception of danger that had to be regulated in
order to be mitigated or removed.

I've already indicated how Thoreau was among the first to recognize
that if Americans continued to view nature itself as the greatest danger
to daily life, the long-term effects would be devastating. As he became
more and more aware of these effects, he began to envision an entirely
different public: a public defined by the danger of losing nature, not
of leaving it to its own devices. Not only would such a public have to
emerge from a different perception of nature and natural beauty, but
it would also have to regulate itself differently. Hence the renowned

passage in "Huckleberries," cited in book after book as an inspiration for the modern environmental movement:

> What are the natural features which make a township handsome—and worth going far to dwell in? A river with its waterfalls—meadows, lakes— hills, cliffs or individual rocks, a forest and single ancient trees—such things are beautiful. They have a high use which dollars and cents never represent. If the inhabitants of a town were wise they would seek to preserve these things though at a considerable expense. For such things educate far more than any hired teachers or preachers, or any at present recognized system of school education.
>
> I do not think him fit to be the founder of a state or even of a town who does not foresee the use of these things, but legislates as it were, for oxen chiefly.
>
> It would be worth the while if in each town there were a committee appointed, to see that the beauty of the town received no detriment. If here is the largest boulder in the country, then it should not belong to an individual nor be made into door-steps. In some countries precious metals belong to the crown—so here more precious objects of great natural beauty should belong to the public.

One of Thoreau's greatest insights was that a part of nature had to remain public for there to be a public of the sort he imagined. That's why his final essays so often treat both unrestrained development and private property as a soul-searing blight upon the land. How, Thoreau wondered, could a nation that split trees into shingles and crushed boulders into doorsteps ever approach a more elevated life in nature? Just to *perceive* the beauty he identified in these essays was in some sense to agree that there might be a moral obligation to protect and conserve nature for its own sake. As the philosopher Martin Heidegger put it in an essay titled "Building Dwelling Thinking", "Saving does not only snatch something from a danger. To save properly means to set something free into its own essence."

Of course, Thoreau realized that a public devoted to protecting as well as improving nature would not arise overnight. People needed to be convinced that if they were willing to take a slightly more adventurous walk, willing to *look* for the natural beauty he had described, they would actually see it. But contrary to the sort of civil disobedience he often advocated, Thoreau also came to believe that unless the obligation to protect and preserve nature could be *enforced*, private interest would prevail no matter what. As much as beauty might open our eyes to nature, some sort of public regulation was needed to preserve it. Without this regulation, there would never truly be a social compact allowing people to gradually approach a life in nature rather than steadily taking leave of it.

When Thoreau died in 1862, leaving his own life in nature to history, he had no way of knowing if his cautionary, subversive comments had hit home. But just three years later things had changed so much that the U.S. Congress voted to cede the Yosemite region to the state of California—making it the first public land preserved solely for public use. Just seven years after that, Yellowstone became the first in a long line of national parks. More than anything, these early efforts to create a national park system showed that the sort of public Thoreau had envisioned was itself being created by the sort of regulations he'd proposed.

Most of what we now think of as the standard template for national parks was first proposed in Frederick Law Olmsted's "Preliminary Report upon the Yosemite and Big Tree Grove" (1865). Commissioned to write the report soon after the Yosemite Grant became law, Olmsted was supposed to make a limited and practical set of recommendations to the governor of California. Instead, he turned it into a more general plea for what Thoreau had called "our national preserves," and just like Thoreau, he began by attacking the rights of private property. "It is the will of the Nation as embodied in the act of Congress that this scenery shall never be private property," Olmsted declared. If "the enjoyment of the choicest natural scenes in the country" is "a monopoly, in a very peculiar manner, of a very few, very rich people," then the need to preserve and protect "great public grounds for the free enjoyment of the people" is both "justified and enforced as a political duty."

What Olmsted felt most duty bound to protect was the region's scenic beauty. "It is in no scene or scenes the charm consists," he writes, "but in the miles of scenery where cliffs of awful height and rocks of vast magnitude and of varied and exquisite coloring, are banked and fringed and draped and shadowed by the tender foliage of noble and lovely trees and bushes." But contrary to the painter Albert Bierstadt and the photographer Carleton Watkins, whom he praises in the report, Olmsted chose to highlight the region's distinctive ecology as well as its scenic views. Notably, he observed that "the difference in the elevation of different parts of the district amounts to considerably more than a mile," making for "a larger number of species of plants within the district than probably can be found within a similar space anywhere else on the continent." This and various other observations meant that Olmsted was among the first to link the preservation of public lands to biodiversity. Above all, he pointed to "the value of the district in its present condition as a museum of natural science and the danger—indeed the certainty—that without care many of the species of plants now flourishing upon it will be lost."

Yet Olmsted also segued fairly quickly from this seminal defense of biodiversity to a discussion of the railroads, bridges, roads, and trails the state would have to build to make the region accessible to "the millions who are hereafter to benefit." As much as he recognized that "an injury to the scenery so slight" that it went "unheeded by any visitor now" could have a "deplorable magnitude" when its effect was multiplied by the millions of visitors to come, he still felt obliged to outline not just a road that would stretch around the valley floor, but a vast network of roads that would stretch all the way to San Francisco. Since almost all the money he asked the state to appropriate was earmarked for infrastructure of one sort or another, this can only mean one thing: that he believed the best way to protect the Yosemite region was by creating a fully engineered landscape that incorporated the region itself as the essential feature. If Yosemite was going to remain *un*developed, in Olmsted's view, it had to be *developed* that way from the start.

Not only did this paradoxical approach shape our view of the national park system, but it has become emblematic of environmentalism as a whole. Bruno Latour is just one of many philosophers and ecologists in recent years to conclude that "Nature, this sacrosanct Nature whose laws should remain 'untouched by human values,' needs our constant care, our undivided attention, our costly instruments, our hundreds of thousands of scientists, our huge institutions, our careful funding." It turns out that the phrase "wilderness management" is not an oxymoron after all. If anything, nature has been *under*-engineered, not *over*engineered—or engineered with the wrong goals in mind. How else are we to understand something like the "Island Civilization"—the "clustering on a planetary scale"—that Roderick Nash has proposed in the latest edition of *Wilderness and the American Mind*? Rather than watching humanity either turn the world into a toxic wasteland or inhabit it so uniformly that wilderness disappears, Nash would like to see several hundred "island" habitats, each about a hundred miles in diameter, surrounded by vast expanses of vacant land that eventually returns to a more pristine state. Plainly, he believes these self-contained zones would make the planet better engineered, but only by turning every inch of it into a global laboratory of sorts: Biosphere 3, perhaps? The "circle of ten miles' radius" that Thoreau called Concord raised to a higher power? The ultimate earthwork?

Sometimes by chance, sometimes by design, Yosemite has been the backdrop to many other aspects of American environmentalism besides Olmsted's "Preliminary Report." John Muir, the Sierra Club, the notorious Hetch Hetchy dam controversy, Ansel Adams's ecological photos, calendars, and posters—all are associated with Yosemite and the surrounding region.

So is a landmark legal case, decided by the U.S. Supreme Court in 1972, which became famous because of Justice William O. Douglas's sensible but stunning dissent. The case, *Sierra Club v. Morton*, reached the Supreme Court because the Sierra Club had strayed onto shaky ground when it sued the U.S. Forest Service for permitting the Disney Corporation to develop a ski resort in a glacial valley called Mineral King. Mineral King is similar in many ways to Yosemite and about a hundred miles south as the crow flies, so it was hardly surprising the Sierra Club led the fight to protect the area.

Like any lawsuit, *Sierra Club v. Morton* had to begin with the issue of legal standing. Since only an injured or endangered party had the right to sue the Forest Service in the first place, the Sierra Club needed to prove it would be harmed in some way by the proposed resort. Unfortunately, and for reasons that are still hard to explain, the organization's brief failed to mention that several of its members lived next to Mineral King and routinely used it for recreational purposes that would be lost if a ski resort were built. The brief actually made it seem as if no member of the Club had even visited the region. That left the Court little choice but to rule against the organization, holding that it inherently lacked standing either as a corporate entity or as a group of individual members.

Douglas's dissent addressed this aspect of the case by noting that what amounted to a technical objection would have been forestalled from the outset if the Sierra Club had simply listed a single member liable to be injured by the ski resort—a point that Justice Potter Stewart, writing for the majority, agreed with in a footnote. This alone made the dissent a legal landmark, since any future plaintiffs in environmental suits of this kind would have to meet a very low threshold for legal standing.

Even so, Douglas's dissent is best known for the way he tried to codify the views of Kant and Thoreau. He actually spent very little time examining the Sierra Club's legal standing. Instead, he kept coming back to the legal standing of *mountains, rivers,* and *lakes,* effectively subordinating the people and organizations who hoped to protect these natural features to the features themselves. A river, Douglas claimed, "speaks for the ecological unit of life that is part of it. Those people who have a meaningful relation to that body of water—whether it be a fisherman, a canoeist, a zoologist, or a logger—must be able to speak for the values which the river represents and which are threatened with destruction." Is it any wonder that he began his dissent by suggesting that the Sierra Club should never have been the plaintiff at all?

> The critical question of "standing" would be simplified and also put neatly in focus if we fashioned a federal rule that allowed environmental issues to be litigated before federal agencies or federal courts in the name of the inanimate object about to be despoiled, defaced, or invaded by roads and bulldozers and where injury is the subject of public outrage. Contemporary public concern for protecting nature's ecological equilibrium should lead to the conferral of standing upon environmental objects to sue for their own preservation. . . . This suit would therefore be more properly labeled as Mineral King v. Morton.

Reading these words more than forty years later, I still find it hard to imagine a better example of what Thoreau had hoped to see. Even now, Douglas's dissent remains one of the most thrilling responses to the aesthetic imperatives that shaped Thoreau's final essays—actually extending or going beyond them by including the inanimate as well as the animate. "The problem," Douglas argued, "is to make certain that the inanimate objects, which are the very core of America's beauty, have spokesmen before they are destroyed." While he didn't believe state and federal agencies were fundamentally venal or corrupt, Douglas did believe they were "notoriously under the control of powerful interests who manipulate them through advisory committees, or friendly working relations, or who have that natural affinity with the agency which in time develops between the regulator and the regulated." The only way to cut through this bureaucratic collusion was to insist that "the voice of the inanimate object" itself "should not be stilled." As Douglas, a big fan of Thoreau, was surely aware, this approach would essentially grant the sort of legal and moral standing to "valleys, alpine meadows, rivers, lakes, estuaries, beaches, ridges, groves of trees, swampland, or even air" that Thoreau had earlier granted the white pine in the essay "Chesuncook." "There is a higher law affecting our relation to pines as well as to men," Thoreau had famously announced. "It is as immortal as I am, and perchance will go to as high a heaven."

Douglas's dissent seems especially significant because even *as* a dissent, a counter friction, it reflected the attitudes of a growing public. We might recall, for instance, that in 1965 Lyndon Johnson became the first president to talk about climate change—and not as a mere myth or something to be denied but as a fact to be faced head on. After a small group of scientific advisers showed him the correlation between rising carbon emissions and rising ocean temperatures (a group that included my father and several colleagues from Scripps Institution of Oceanography), Johnson warned the American public that "this generation has altered the composition of the atmosphere on a global scale through radioactive materials and a steady increase in carbon dioxide from the burning of fossil fuels." The warning was even more notable because it appeared in a "Special Message to the Congress on Conservation and Restoration of Natural Beauty." This was the prologue to a White House Conference on National Beauty—chaired by Laurance Rockefeller twenty years before he donated the land for the state preserve that my wife and I enjoy so much.

Though it took someone like Justice Douglas to connect the dots once and for all, the "Special Message" was just one of many indications that Americans were now willing, and even felt a duty, to protect nature for something more than its usefulness or its scenic qualities alone. The Clean Air Act had been passed in 1963 and the Wilderness Act in 1964, just the first of many environmental regulations Congress approved during the next decade. Between 1960 and 1970, membership in the Sierra Club rose from 16,000 to 114,000; in 1970, Americans celebrated the first Earth Day and Richard Nixon authorized the Environmental Protection Agency; in 1971, Greenpeace was founded; in 1972, Disney decided not to build the resort at Mineral King, which later became part of Sequoia National Park; and in 1973, Congress passed the Endangered

Species Act, putting into place what Edward O. Wilson has called "the most important conservation law in the history of the United States."

Of course, Wilson soon gave the moral and aesthetic impulse to conserve nature a new name: *biophilia*. Psychologist Erich Fromm originally defined *biophilia* as a "love of life or living systems." Wilson, the biologist, slightly modified the term in the mid-1980s to mean an "innate tendency to focus on life and lifelike processes." But because life as a whole seems to have no value or purpose other than life itself, Wilson eventually concluded that biophilia would be better defined as the "innately emotional affiliation of human beings to other living organisms." What he meant by this was that biophilia is inherently moral. It was his way of saying that "existential conservatism"—"the preservation of biological human nature as a sacred trust"—can never be separated from the duty to protect all of biological nature.

Though Wilson now regards biophilia as an evolutionary trait of human beings, he's the first to admit that our *awareness* of this trait probably owes more to Thoreau's swampy, sympathetic view of nature than to any other single factor. The journal alone is filled with entry after entry indicating how thoroughly Thoreau identified with nature, among them "There is, no doubt, a perfect analogy between the life of the human being and that of the vegetable, both of the body and the mind" and "The mystery of the life of plants is kindred to that of our own lives." Only someone who held this view of life would have begun the essay "Walking" by announcing, "I wish to speak a word for Nature, for absolute freedom and wildness, as contrasted with a freedom and culture merely civil,—to regard man as an inhabitant, or a part and parcel of Nature, rather than a member of society." Likewise, only someone who held this view would have said that we're always "reading our own physical and corresponding moral revolutions" when we study nature, that the *mere perception* of natural beauty is a moral test. Not only was Thoreau the first to say these things, but his memorable, aphoristic style has made them hard to forget.

That Thoreau kept coming back to the moral feelings associated with natural beauty may be the most enduring aspect of his environmental imagination. If the ongoing struggle to address global warming is any indication, people are no longer willing to rely on the sort of accumulating evidence that my father and the other scientists who advised Lyndon

Johnson assumed was reason enough to start taking precautions. They believed that an "is" inevitably implied an "ought"—or, in the words of the climatologist Dale Jamieson, that a set of values or priorities could "simply be read from the science." In fact, this wasn't even true at the time, at least not among those who misjudged the scale or the urgency of the threat. Jamieson recounts that when one scientist informed a congressional committee in 1965 that atmospheric CO_2 would have a huge impact on the environment by 2015, he was politely received, politely dismissed, and told to report back to the committee in 2014.

Every environmental crisis begs the question of how we interpret the science that defines it. Indeed, almost any crisis can begin as a crisis of objectivity—leading Latour, for one, to suggest that when facts become the final arbitrator of a crisis, the debate about it is actually "short-circuited." Whether you agree with Latour or not, the opposite has been true of global warming: the greater the factual evidence for global warming, the more a number of people have chosen to *disbelieve* the facts. Jamieson is merely stating the obvious when he says that many segments of American society today see "nothing wrong with accepting evidence based on their beliefs rather than accepting beliefs based on the evidence." A rising sea level may be slowly, steadily, and *visibly* flooding the low-lying streets of Miami Beach, but Governor Rick Scott has told Florida's Department of Environmental Protection not to use the words "climate change" or "global warming" in any of its reports.

That's why both Jamieson and Latour believe the perception of environmental danger is less about facts than values. Just as the abortion debate has really been about human rights, not the growing ability of science to detect birth defects or keep younger and younger babies alive, so the global warming debate has been about human and nonhuman rights, not the mere regulation of carbon emissions or the need to develop wind turbines and solar panels. We've actually reached the point where a number of activists worry that the issue of global warming is so big that it's unintentionally sucking the air out of more local and regional efforts to protect the environment—making these efforts seem less urgent, less important, less worth funding. How can saving the yellow-billed cuckoo, the cave beetle, or the Florida prairie-clover compare to saving the world? The answer we give is more likely to depend on our values than the certainty or uncertainty of environmental science being able to solve the problem. In the end, we all have an environmental ethic of some sort, even those who think of nature as an industrial site, not a park or preserve. Teddy Roosevelt may have been one of the most avid conservationists in the nation's history, but he was also a lethal and insatiable big-game hunter. Whenever he heard the word nature he reached for his gun.

Instead of a stuffed head or two, mounted glassy-eyed and immobile on his attic wall, Thoreau put together a *living* collection of plants and animals that moved and changed with each walk he took. One day he happened upon a crimson pincushion gall, the next day he scented a white water lily that "burst up so pure and fair to the eye" that it revealed "what purity and sweetness reside in, and can be extracted from, the slime and muck of earth." Thoreau was interested in the "analogy" that existed between himself and nature, not the sort of predatory behavior that put him at odds with it. Though he had an exacting eye, the glass he used to magnify nature was ground far more to Kant's specifications than Darwin or Locke's. A journal entry from 1851 reads, "How important is a constant intercourse with nature and the contemplation of natural phenomenon to the preservation of moral and intellectual health!" He is even more ardent in the passage that appears toward the end of *A Week on the Concord and Merrimack Rivers* in which he first announces his desire to live a life in nature: "Men nowhere, east or west, live yet a *natural* life, round which the vine clings, and which the elm willingly shadows. Man would desecrate it by his touch, and so the beauty of the world remains veiled to him. He needs not only to be spiritualized, but *naturalized*, on the soil of the earth."

We would do well ourselves to view nature through a glass of Kant's making. With everything we know about evolution and genetics these days, the distinction between the human and the nonhuman is smaller than it's ever been. Fossils found in East Africa during the 1960s and '70s proved that humans and apes evolved from a common ancestor; more recently, genetic sequencing has shown that we also share a majority of our genes with mice and fruit flies. Ultimately, all species great and small can be seen as analogous to us. And yet our view of the nonhuman remains as queasy, as puritanical, and as dismissive as ever. There are so many trees in my neighborhood with limbs knocked off by passing trucks that the sight of a crudely painted sign—"Trees are human too!"—seems almost laughably out of place. Sometimes I have to will myself to see the beauty that exists here anyway, the beauty that Thoreau alluded to when he said, "Such is beauty ever,—neither here nor there, now nor then,—neither in Rome nor in Athens, but wherever there is a soul to admire."

Thoreau looked to beauty to demonstrate that our analogous relation to nature is *always* a moral choice. But even this was a kind of analogy, since he generally made his point by asking people to choose the *meaning* of natural beauty at the same time. Saying that the scenery of Walden was "on a humble scale" forced people to look at the pond differently, forced them to *choose* to look at it differently, see what made it beautiful in Thoreau's eyes and what might make it beautiful in theirs. Though a better scientific understanding of the pond could add to its beauty, or help to reveal its beauty in the first place, Thoreau kept reminding people that there was always something *more* to see, always something even *more* beautiful, if they were prepared to go beyond what they expected to see and looked at things with a new and different intention of the eye. "There is just as much beauty visible to us in the landscape as we are prepared to appreciate,—not a grain more."

When Thoreau said, "In Wildness is the preservation of the world," he wasn't simply taking wildness for granted. Wildness is actually his greatest test of our capacity for moral choice. After all, beauty itself is neither innocent nor naïve. Anyone familiar with the history of Indian removal in America knows how often Native Americans were called ugly, dirty, and depraved. Like the Salem witch trials or the Puritan rule that farmers had to clear all "Swampes and such Rubbish waest grounds" within three years, Indian removal was an act of aesthetic purification. The Fascists of the 1920s were willing to push this craving for ethnic and political purity to such lengths that Walter Benjamin said humanity seemed ready to "experience its own destruction as an aesthetic pleasure of the first order." The same thing could be said of those who believe that humans are so fatal to nature that the only way to save the world is by getting rid of us. "Back to the Pleistocene!" the slogan reads.

But wildness is a hybrid, half-breed, open-ended aesthetic that symbolizes Thoreau's evolving analogy between the human and the nonhuman. Wildness is beauty in a democratic form—a form in which the human and the nonhuman are not just equivalent but equal, endowed with the same rights and privileges and subject to the same laws of nature that Thomas Jefferson referred to in the Declaration of Independence. Wildness is Caliban released from servitude and seen in the light of genetic engineering and biophilia; it's Arachne's sentence commuted to the sort of glinting gossamer web that Thoreau described as being "of the finest conceivable texture" and "made to strain the air and light"; it's Thoreau's appreciation for the "transcendent and dazzling beauty" of the pickerel in Walden Pond, his effort to see them as "the pearls of Walden, some animalized Walden water," rather than his next meal.

No one before or since Thoreau has been more attuned to the moral obligations of natural beauty. For many American environmentalists in particular, his is the still, small voice that will forever reverberate in our heads. "By the mediation of a thousand little mosses and fungi, the most unsightly objects become radiant of beauty," he writes in the journal. By asking us to look for this radiant beauty ourselves, he transformed the act of seeing into an act of wide-eyed appreciation and choice. Imagine how much less we would see of nature's boundless beauty without his writings. Imagine how much less we would elect to protect. Like the Roman politician of Cicero's day, Thoreau was unable to save himself without saving the rest of the country as well.

Conclusion

Mormon Mesa is a flat, arid wedge of land about sixty-five miles northeast of Las Vegas. It rises between the Virgin River and the Muddy River, which meet at an oblique angle to form the apex of the dry wedge before draining into Lake Mead, the largest artificial lake in the United States. The top of the mesa is covered with a layer of loose, weathered caliche cobbles—a sedimentary rock bound together by calcium carbonate. Scattered over the cobbles are clumps of creosote and white bursage, spaced far enough apart to drive a car between, but also numerous enough to give the area an olive-green cast at eye level. During the mid-1800s, the mesa was crossed by the Old Spanish Trail, a trade route stretching from Santa Fe to Los Angeles, with the distance between the two rivers representing a single day's *jornada* on the trail—water to water. Now I-15 cuts across it to the north and the entire tableland is veined by dirt roads running diagonally or at right angles to each other.

Not long ago my wife and I rented a car in Las Vegas and drove to Mormon Mesa. Fearing that cell phone reception might be iffy, I had printed out a map and directions. But as we made our way past the Overton airport and up and onto the mesa, what looked clear on the map looked less clear on the ground. As soon as a fairly straight stretch of road petered out, we got confused and found ourselves headed down a steep and rutted route to the valley seventeen hundred feet below. Only after we stopped and backed our way to the top again did we figure out where we were—at which point we began to wind along a wispy, sometimes indistinct road that closely skirted the canyon rims cutting into the mesa on either side. We were beginning to get a bit edgy when I nearly drove us into what we'd come to see all along: a large earthwork called *Double Negative*, completed by the artist Michael Heizer in 1970.

Double Negative was one of the first earthworks to be created when the land art movement arose during the late 1960s, and along with

Robert Smithson's *Spiral Jetty* in Utah, Walter De Maria's *Lightning Field* (1977) in New Mexico, and James Turrell's *Roden Crater* (begun 1977) in Arizona, it remains one of the most renowned. Over the years, *Double Negative* has been written about many times, photographed countless times, and, if only as a straight and rather mysterious cast shadow, is easily big enough to be seen on Google Earth. While poring over these various images and descriptions, I had visited the sculpture many times in my imagination. But not until my wife and I saw it in person, *experienced* it in person, did I fully understand what makes it so special.

Heizer constructed the iconic work by bulldozing two ditches 30 feet wide and 50 feet deep, each with 45-degree ramps and 90-degree walls, forming two halves of a sculpture—already a kind of double negative— which stretches across the open or negative space of a rather wide but shallow canyon. Standing within the walls of one ditch and facing the other across the yawning gap, it's as if the very idea of space has been rendered positive by what's missing—much like two mirrors turned face to face. "There's nothing there," Heizer has remarked, "yet it is still a sculpture." Transfixed by the sublime possibilities of positive and negative space, he not only created a compelling work of art, but turned a naturally extant void, framed by a mechanized cut-out on either side, into a stark, decisive, and alluring feature of the landscape.

All of this can be seen in a photograph or grasped as a concept. What you have to see firsthand is how perfectly Heizer has scaled *Double Negative* to the human body and to the surrounding landforms. De Maria once said, "I don't think art can stand up to nature. Put the best object you know next to the grand canyon, niagara falls, the red woods. The big things always win." But size has always differed from scale and Heizer's work is so well proportioned that it's neither belittled nor dwarfed by its surroundings. If anything, it turns the immense scale of Mormon Mesa into a plus, not a minus. Certainly, the bottoms of the two ditches, their high walls as enclosed and claustrophobic as the sheer vertical sides of any river-cut gulch, have been slanted to the open space between them so nicely that the magnitude of the separation makes you feel ecstatic once you stand on its verge.

Of course, sculpture is routinely said to be "about" space. But the space *Double Negative* creates is of a different magnitude than most sculpture. In effect, Heizer wants people to appreciate the magnitude of space itself—something we're dimly aware of at times, especially west of the Mississippi, but without necessarily *feeling* it so directly and intensely or believing that it really *matters* for its own sake. He was aware that the desert in particular had long been considered a null or negative space, within both the Anglo-American landscape tradition and the modernist tradition of art. Where it wasn't overlooked or ignored, it was avoided. But Heizer excavated this absent sphere so deeply and decisively that *Double Negative* has now become a site many people feel they can't miss seeing. Even as my wife and I were leaving, two ATVs pulled up with two new groups of pilgrims. For all of us, hollowed ground was now hallowed ground.

Almost all earthworks come stamped with an expiration date. Very few are as short-lived as Dennis Oppenheim's *Accumulation Cut* (1968), where the artist used a chainsaw to cut a narrow trench through a layer of lake ice that froze again in twenty-four hours. But even the most durable works have usually been constructed in remote places and abandoned to the forces of wind, frost, and water. *Double Negative* is already so eroded that my wife and I had to pick our way around large chunks of fallen rock to reach the bottom of each ditch, and the crisply cut, right-angled walls are now sagging and seamed. It may not be long before the cut grooves are mere gullies and the work itself ceases to exist.

Much the same thing is true of *Spiral Jetty*. When Smithson built the *Jetty*, he failed to factor in the way the waters of the Great Salt Lake rise in wet years and fall in dry years—and, as chance would have it, he leveled the work just high enough to clear the water line of a dry year. Since then, the *Jetty* has been more submerged than exposed. Indeed, when we were thinking of visiting the work a few years ago, I was directed to a website that allows you to calculate if the work is above or below the current water level. Happily, it was high and dry at the time. Yet once we set foot on the *Jetty* and began following its inward path, we realized the rocks we were walking on were so encrusted with salt crystals that they might soon be buried when not submerged.

I always feel anguished when thinking about this entropic arc—this aesthetic version of earth to earth, dust to dust. For me, it represents something lost. But I know that for many others the end can't come soon enough. Earthworks have had a particularly rocky relationship to the environmental movement. Mostly, they've been a lightning rod for those who would like to exile humanity from nature once and for all: the "Back to the Pleistocene!" wing of the movement. They've also upset those who believe the country's more remote deserts and forests represent an original state of nature, along with those who want to clean up old mining and industrial sites by restoring them to an original state of nature.

As already noted, Smithson, relishing the role of provocateur, made a special point of ridiculing the sort of people who wished to return "to Paradise or 19th century landscape which is basically what the conservationist attitude is." Indeed, Smithson seemed to put as much distance as he could between himself and the nineteenth century. But this distance was mainly an expression of the "ecological despair" he felt in the face of "metaphysical" "modern day ecologists" who usually saw "the operations of industry as Satan's work" and whose "image of the lost paradise garden" left them floundering in romantic fictions. Just before his death, Smithson published an article in which he bluntly stated that Olmsted's design for Central Park made him America's first earthwork artist. Since Central Park was the prototype for a fully engineered—or what Smithson himself called a "dialectical"—landscape, he clearly considered his aesthetic to be an extension, a reflection, and ultimately a self-cancelling mirror image of the landscape that so many others were trying to sentimentalize in absentia. Referring to a "before" photograph of the "man-made wasteland" in the middle of Manhattan that Olmsted "would remake in terms of earth sculpture," Smithson impudently remarked, "It reminds me of the strip-mining regions I saw last year in southeastern Ohio."

_____

I wish I could say that Smithson's sharp-edged remarks weren't still furrowing brows. But many environmentalists remain baffled by works like *Double Negative* and *Spiral Jetty*; either that, or they accuse them of being frivolous, elitist, arrogant, or reactionary—not just an eyesore but actually harmful to the sites they disrupt in the name of art. Even those who are sympathetic can be skeptical at times. The critic Lucy Lippard has long been a champion of land art, contributing some of the most knowledgeable and insightful accounts of these works over the past few decades. But in 2014 she wrote a book entitled *Undermining* in which she explains that moving to New Mexico has made her take a step backward from the movement. Using the extraction of gravel to show how mining companies have turned the natural geology of her state into a network of concrete highways and bridges, Lippard admits that "the politics of land use have replaced land art" in her mind's eye. Not surprisingly, only Smithson still interests her. Among other things, she's distressed that "land art tends to be site-specific but not overtly place-specific," ignoring a history of land use that has long included Native Americans and Spanish Americans. She even refers to land art as "a kind of colonization in itself."

Though I have no quarrel with this, I keep coming back to what it's like to experience a work like *Double Negative*. Take the way it enlarges our sense of scale. The environmental movement has been plagued by the low-profile, naked-eye scale of everyday life. As Dale Jamieson recently noted in his study of why the effort to scale back climate change remains so feeble, human beings are engineered to respond to the rapid movements of middle-sized objects in the middle distance, not the slow buildup of invisible gases. Because we're unable to *sense* the scale of climate change, we're also insensitive to how urgently we need to address it. Both of these things show how limited we are by the sort of epistemology Locke described in his *Essay concerning Human Understanding*.

But *Double Negative* deliberately disregards the middle distance, asking us to experience the fullness of Earth from *within*—both literally and sensibly from within—before making our way toward a wide-open canyon that provokes a *global* sense of withinness. Personally, I found this experience liberating, at least in part because space seemed more pressing, more crucial to the way I looked at the world.

Standing on the bottom of the ditch I had nearly driven our car into, the sky a narrow sliver of blue above, I felt enclosed by the earth and by the earth alone. The walls rising so near and high forced me to examine them up close, not as some object vaguely evident in the middle distance or far away. I reached out to touch their crumbling surface. I smelled their dusty particles, felt them in my eyes and on my skin. Looking down, I noticed that some of the earth beneath my feet was fine enough to have been sifted, while the rest was grainy, caked, and hard. Looking around, I observed that a number of sage bushes had taken root and that the fallen boulders had left the walls pocked, with the promise of more ruin to come. Gradually, a negative space became positive—not empty but full of incident and effect.

As I walked out of the ditch and stood on an apron of land that had been bulldozed flat, the sweeping canyon at my feet emerged as yet another negative space, uniting the narrow opening Heizer had hollowed out with the vastly larger expanse of earth itself. The abrupt contrast between the two spaces was both disconcerting and intoxicating at the same time. Heizer understood that a background isn't a background without a foreground. He knew that infinity is best perceived from where we stand. But he also knew that we have to be made *aware* of where we stand. I would never have cleaved to that open expanse so strongly if I hadn't faced such a confined space just before. Yet because the two halved ditches turned out to span a broad canyon, matter suddenly melted into air and the local morphed into the global—earth became Earth. It reminded me that Smithson and Heizer were among the many land artists inspired by astronaut William Anders's astonishing photo of the half-shadowed Earth, suspended aqueous and beckoning against the dark nothingness of space and the moon's grey monochrome, taken during the Apollo 8 mission in 1968. *Earthrise*, indeed.

I've found it helpful to think about Heizer's *Double Negative* by comparing it to Thoreau's description of the Deep Cut excavated by the Fitchburg Railroad the year before he moved to the pond. Appearing in the "Spring" chapter of *Walden*, this memorable description is one of Thoreau's most exalted and sympathetic accounts of nature. Yet the site itself is no less invasive or artificial than Heizer's. Indeed, Thoreau's introductory words seem very much like something Smithson or Heizer might have written to explain their own work: "Few phenomena give me more delight than to observe the forms which thawing sand and clay assume in flowing down the sides of a deep cut on the railroad through which I passed on my way to the village, a phenomenon not very common on so large a scale, though the number of freshly exposed banks of the right material must have been greatly multiplied since railroads were invented."

What follows is a brilliant convergence of the animate and the inanimate, all activated by a thaw in which the sand has begun "to flow down the slopes like lava." "Innumerable little streams" of sand "overlap and interlace one with another," Thoreau observes, "exhibiting a sort of hybrid product, which obeys half way the law of currents, and half way that of vegetation"—"a sort of architectural foliage more ancient and typical than acanthus, chicory, ivy, vine, or any vegetable leaves; destined

Herbert Wendell Gleason, *Sand foliage from Deep Cut on R.R., Concord, Mass., March 17, 1900.* Courtesy of Concord Free Public Library.

perhaps, under some circumstances, to become a puzzle to future geologists." Smithson, who was no less sensitive to the matched materiality of words and things, couldn't have said it better himself. As a matter of fact, Thoreau might have been putting words in Smithson's mouth when he said, "The earth is not a mere fragment of dead history, stratum upon stratum like the leaves of a book, to be studied by geologists and antiquaries chiefly, but living poetry like the leaves of a tree, which precede flowers and fruit,—not a fossil earth, but a living earth." Certainly, both Smithson and Heizer could agree with Thoreau that "this one hillside illustrated the principle of all the operations of Nature."

Any disagreement among the three would be over the principle itself. Smithson and Heizer chose to work with backhoes and bulldozers

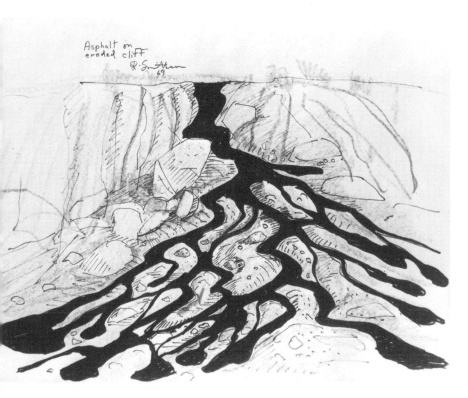

Robert Smithson, *Asphalt on Eroded Cliff*, 1969. Pencil and ink on paper, dimensions unknown. Courtesy of James Cohan, New York. Art © Holt-Smithson Foundation/ Licensed by VAGA, New York, N.Y.

because their guiding metaphors and materials were mineral, not vegetable. Earth was hard, so to speak, not soft. Lava halted and hardened rather than flowing on, and they were more apt to gouge it than grow something in it. Thoreau, on the other hand, typically chose to evoke the fleshy leaves of a deciduous maple or oak. As he says, and echoes throughout his writings, "You find thus in the very sands an anticipation of the vegetable leaf. No wonder that the earth expresses itself outwardly in leaves, it so labors with the idea inwardly. The atoms have already learned this law, and are pregnant by it. The overhanging leaf sees here its prototype."

Still, Thoreau would never have seen the leaf in this light if he didn't think it had the same sort of scalability, the same sort of *self-similarity*, that Smithson and Heizer relied on as well. To be sure, the actual theory of self-similarity was little known before the mid-1970s and Smithson and Heizer were probably as ignorant of it as Thoreau. But all three seemed to understand the theory intuitively—Thoreau, in particular, because one of the easiest ways to understand self-similarity is to imagine a tree.

As a geometric shape, a tree is nothing more than a series of branches. But it's a series that looks more or less the same at every point, from the newest, smallest, most delicate branches at the ends of the outermost limbs to the largest branches rising out of the main trunk of the tree. The tree grows by reproducing this shape over and over again, and thus the whole has approximately the same shape as each of its parts. Another way of putting this is that the tree is symmetrical at every scale—which is exactly what Thoreau means when he says, "It is wonderful how rapidly yet perfectly the sand organizes itself as it flows, using the best material its mass affords to form the sharp edges of its channel. Such are the sources of rivers. In the silicious matter which the water deposits is perhaps the bony system, and in the still finer soil and organic matter the fleshy fibre or cellular tissue."

Thoreau seems even more aligned with Smithson and Heizer when he describes the deeply scalloped shape of the scarlet oak leaf in "Autumnal Tints," toggling back and forth between the positive and negative space of land and water. "Regarded as water," he notes, the leaf "is like a pond with half a dozen broad rounded promontories extending nearly to its middle, half from each side, while its watery bays extend far inland," forming "a leafy archipelago." Yet it "oftener suggests land, and, as Dionysius and Pliny compared the form of the Morea to that of the leaf of the Oriental Plane-tree, so this leaf reminds me of some fair wild island in the ocean," marked by an "extensive coast, alternate rounded bays with smooth strands, and sharp-pointed rocky capes."

Not only did Thoreau equate botany and geology, but he saw this morphological equation holding steady at every scale. To stand in the melting sands of the Deep Cut was to stand in the furrow of a ploughed field and the bottom of the Grand Canyon all at once. Essentially, the entire world lay within its sharply angled walls. True, Thoreau often felt as if the walls "were turned wrong side outwards." But that's just another reason to compare the Deep Cut to Heizer's *Double Negative*.

Nor is this the only comparison that comes to mind. Even as land art arose in the 1960s, there was a countervailing effort to explore the more organic or biological aspects of nature. One of the earliest of these artworks was Hans Haacke's *Condensation Cube*, created in 1962. As its name suggests, the piece was a closed Plexiglas box with enough water in the bottom to create "a delicate veil" of condensation as the box heated up in sunlight. In Haacke's description, "The drops grow—hour by hour—small ones combine with larger ones. The speed of growth depends on the intensity and the angle of the intruding light. After a day, a dense cover of clearly defined drops has developed and they all reflect light. With continuing condensation, some drops reach such a size that their weight overcomes the forces of adhesion and they run down along the walls"—leaving the sort of living "trace" that Thoreau perceived in the melting sands.

Other artworks have been bolder or more extreme. In 1965, Alan Sonfist proposed his *Time Landscape*, a nearly block-long strip of dirt, planted with species native to precolonial New York, that would transition from grasses to full-grown trees. The work was finally completed in 1978 and still exists just north of Soho in Manhattan. I've passed it many times over the years, monitoring how most of the grasses died out as the trees rose and their spreading branches gradually cut down the amount of sunlight reaching the ground. But I've also seen a number of flowering plants spring up, their petals and leaves reaching through the metal bars of the fenced area.

In 1982, Agnes Denes took a more ironic and transitory approach to botany, planting a field of nonindigenous wheat in a lower-Manhattan landfill that soon gave way to the towering buildings of Battery Park City. *Wheatfield* was a poignant and beautiful environment while it was there—a rectangle of life in the midst of rubble. As it grew taller, I was reminded that there are other ways of feeling lifted by the wind than by seeing loose trash swirling in the air; as it grew riper, I lost myself in its promise of fullness. When the field was eventually harvested it became a symbolic source of seeds used to protest world hunger—an action I saw as an updated version of Dennis Oppenheim's *Directed Seeding/Cancelled Crop*, where a field in northern Holland was "planted and cultivated for the sole purpose of withholding it from a product-oriented system."

A decade later, Mel Chin created *Revival Field*, a work in which he planted not just a small area of landfill, but an actual Superfund site in St. Paul, Minnesota, with the sort of "'hyper-accumulator' plants" that "can pull metals out of the soil into their stems and leaves." During an interview Chin said, "The revived ecological system that is created from sculpting away toxins from million of tons of polluted earth—that is the 'aesthetic product.' Something that has potential for death or injury because of chemical and industrial practices is brought back to life using something that is found naturally—that is the sculpture."

That was also the year that several other artists began to move in a more radical and controversial direction—dabbling in the possibilities of genetic engineering. A rather innocuous example was David Kremers's Somite series, begun in 1992, in which he manipulated some colorless bacteria to react to certain dye compounds. Once this reaction produced a number of vibrant "paintings," as Kremers referred to them, he sealed the bacteria's "agar-covered acrylic plates" in synthetic resin—arresting any further growth but leaving the bacteria themselves stable and alive. A more ominous example, from 2000, was Eduardo Kac's misguided effort to implant an albino rabbit with a synthesized version of the two proteins that cause crystal jellyfish to flash a fluorescent green—hoping to create a living, breathing, nonradioactive version of a glow-in-the-dark toy. Fortunately, the lab he was working with in France got cold feet and closed the experiment down.

I don't think this will be the fate of Joe Davis's far more playful plan to create a *Tree of Knowledge*. Several years ago, Davis announced that he had received the roots and leaves of a four-thousand-year-old strain of apple, and that he intended to insert a coded version of Wikipedia into the ancient apple (genus name *Malus*, meaning both "bad, evil," and "apple tree" in Latin, an etymology Thoreau would have been aware of, too, when he made so much of wild apples). The tree will actually be a forest, because each bacterium Davis plans to use in the process can carry only a portion of Wikipedia's two and a half billion words, forcing him to divide them among a multitude of trees. But in the words of Patrick House, whose short article about the project in the *New Yorker* has become the chief source of information about it, "the engineered apple, when complete, will be twice forbidden—the Animal and Plant Health Inspection Service of the U.S. Department of Agriculture" having instituted "strict rules against the unregulated eating of genetically altered plants."

I believe each of these more recent, more microscopic cuts can be related to the deep cuts excavated by both Heizer and the Fitchburg Railroad. But the genomic project that most interests me is poet Christian Bök's equally provocative *Xenotext Experiment*. Though Bök has generally been associated with the tradition of disinterested, "uncreative" art that includes Marcel Duchamp, John Cage, Andy Warhol, and Kenneth Goldsmith, his decision to genetically engineer this tradition has given it new life.

Bök's first book of poetry, *Crystallography*, sets out to show that "a word is a bit of crystal in formation," and as a basic concept it reminds me a lot of Smithson's obsession with enantiomorphic quartz crystals and Thoreau's notion of crystalline botany. Bök's second book, *Eunoia*, is divided into five sections, each restricted to a single vowel, and each written using only that vowel—as in "I bitch; I kibbitz—griping whilst criticizing dimwits, sniping whilst indicting nitwits, dismissing simplistic thinking, in which philippic wit is still illicit." *Eunoia*'s enforced rigor comes across as a study in how language is able to survive under the most narrow or severe conditions, creating an odd likeness to the biological organisms known as extremophiles that are able to survive almost anywhere.

The *Xenotext Experiment* pushes this likeness much further. Simply put, for the past decade or so Bök has been trying to genetically engineer *Deinococcus radiodurans*—the extremophilic bacterium par excellence—into what he calls a biological "poetry machine." *D. radiodurans* has proved so immune to acid, radiation, dehydration, moisture, and intense heat or cold that it's been found in everything from llama feces to Antarctic rock formations and an irradiated can of pork. If Bök can transform the bacterium into a "living poem," it will be the genetic equivalent of the "living earth" Thoreau discovered in the melting-sand-poetry of the Deep Cut. Language will literally come alive. And it may last as long as Earth lasts.

Of course, Thoreau was also obsessed with language, not just in the way he played with words, but more explicitly in the Deep Cut description where he explores the foliating etymology of *leaf*. "*Internally*," Thoreau explains—after equating the leafy prototype with both the "foliaceous mass" of the sands and the "vitals of the animal body"—"it is a moist thick *lobe*, a word especially applicable to the liver and lungs and the leaves of fat, (λείβω, *labor, lapsus*, to flow or slip downward, a lapsing;

λοβός, *globus*, lobe, globe; also lap, flap, and many other words,) *externally*, a dry thin *leaf*, even as the *f* and *v* are a pressed and dried *b*. The radicals of *lobe* are *lb*, the soft mass of the *b* (single lobed, or B, double lobed,) with the liquid *l* behind it pressing it forward." When he also says, "I am affected as if in a peculiar sense I stood in the laboratory of the Artist who made the world and me," it seems pretty clear that he saw the leaf, too, as a form of living poetry. That he discovered this poetry in an arenaceous laboratory created by the Fitchburg Railroad didn't bother him in the least.

Still, Bök takes the notion of linguistic engineering to a different level—cutting even deeper into nature, adding even more to the romantic ideal of artists being able to mimic the creativity of Nature. When he first announced the *Xenotext* project, Bök said he was "trying to write a book of poetry in which I translate a single poem, through a process of encipherment, into a sequence of genetic nucleotides." He indicated that he planned to build a "genetic sequence in a laboratory so that I can implant the gene into a bacterium, replacing a portion of its genome with my text. The bacterium would, in effect, *be* the poem." He quickly amended this, however, to suggest that the bacterium would be more like "a machine for writing a poem" *in response* to a poem of his own that he'd implant. Since the bacterium had to "read" his poem to begin with, Bök needed to "write" it by translating each letter of the alphabet into a codon—a "triplet" of DNA nucleotides—combining and recombining adenine (A), cytocine (C), guanine (G), and thymine (T). For instance, the letter *A* might be coded as ACT, *B* might be coded as AGT, *C* might be coded as CGT, and so on. But Bök believed that by implanting a poem in this way, by cutting into the bacterium's genome, *D. radiodurans* would produce a protein that was "yet another poem."

More than a decade later, he's still looking for a response from *D. radiodurans*. But in the meantime, he's successfully engineered an *Escherichia coli* bacterium, a run-of-the-mill organism that's present in the intestines of most warm-blooded animals, but probably best known as the cause of so many Food and Drug Administration warnings and recalls. In 2011, after a steady year of work on his "poetic cypher, gene X-P13," Bök reported that he'd implanted the lines "any style of life/is prim" into the genome of an *E. coli* bacterium, and that it had "fluoresced red," or "answered," with the lines "the faery is rosy/of glow." Though this limited response sequence may fall short of Bök's final goal, it goes way beyond the "watermarks" that many genetic engineering companies insert in the genomes they synthesize. Using codon sequences to spell out the company's name or list the names of the scientists who worked on a project is hardly the same thing as "reading" these names and "writing" a new list.

In 2015, in what looks like a kind of hardcopy update, Bök published *The Xenotext: Book 1*. It's both a genetic primer and an eclectic, illustrated collection of poems inspired by his latest linguistic constraint, the structure of amino acids. But everything in it is magnified by the global environmental crisis. The opening prose poem, "The Late Heavy Bombardment," asks, "What Great Comet has yet to plummet from the heavens, like a rocket engine dousing its jets during splashdown in your oceans of nitroglycerine? What thunderclap has yet to herald the advent of this plowshare, which can bulldoze a mountain into rubble upon impact? What match-heads, when scraped against your atmosphere, can ignite its oxygen, turning the sky into a blazing typhoon?" A much longer poem is devoted to the still unexplained "colony collapse" of bees around the world.

If this apocalyptic tone sounds familiar, I'm inclined to say it's because the poems so often resemble Smithson's ornery, overheated, science-fictionalized style. Since Bök is familiar with Smithson's writings, and both owe a debt to William S. Burroughs's Nova Trilogy and Jorge Luis Borges's Library of Babel, I'd also have to say that the environmental aesthetic stretching from Thoreau's description of the Deep Cut to the earthworks of Smithson and Heizer lives on in the work of Bök and various other artists and writers working at a genetic scale. By working smaller, these artists have created their own deep cuts—but at the scale of all life on earth.

Like it or not, Thoreau's description of the Deep Cut, Heizer's *Double Negative*, and Bök's *Xenotext Experiment* cut to the core of modern environmentalism. William Wordsworth once remarked, "Why take pains to prove that an Ape is not a Newton when it is self-evident that he is not a man." Similarly, why object to nature being overrun by humans when it has never existed as such without us? Nature is a human invention, shown over and over again by cultures that have no word for the object that modern science calls "wilderness" or "nature." In *Beyond Nature and*

Culture, Philippe Descola recounts that when a section of Jawoyn land in northern Australia was set aside as a national park, a tribal leader responded by saying that the territory was "not a wilderness" but "a human artefact"—"a land constructed by us over tens of thousands of years through our ceremonies and ties of kinship, through fire and through hunting." Carleton Watkins made the same mistake in the early 1860s when he photographed Yosemite Valley—fancying its wild and open meadows to be the work of nature instead of generations of fires set by the Miwok peoples. Maybe it's time for us to think of "nature" as a synonym for "the Anthropocene."

Clearly, Smithson was right to say that "a kind of 'virgin' beauty was established in the early days of this country and most people who don't look too hard tend to see the world through postcards and calendars so that that affects their idea of what they think nature should be rather than what it is." To generalize his point, those who insist that the birth of the Anthropocene signifies the death of nature are trafficking in values, not facts. I assume values will also determine if the Anthropocene itself is expansively equated with what geologists now call the Holocene or narrowed to a more recent period—the rise of the Industrial Revolution, say, or everything after the first atom bomb test. But no matter what, Thoreau's luminous description of the Deep Cut—its machined yet yielding banks the very picture of nature to his joyfully hybridized eye—makes me believe that American *environmentalism* began with the thawing sands *above* Walden Pond as well as the undisturbed sands beneath its waters.

Environmental works like *Walden*, the *Xenotext Experiment*, and *Double Negative* effectively align art and ethics—prompting a heightened moral awareness by bringing us to our senses in new and different ways. All of these works push the aesthetic boundaries of art. All of them prove that art can not only stand up to nature but actually *be* nature. And all of them force us to ask ourselves, *should* nature be this way? Whether we choose to see these works as good or bad, examples or counterexamples, their aesthetic urgency goes hand in hand with their moral urgency. They cut both ways. And they keep on cutting . . .

ACKNOWLEDGMENTS

In one way or another, a number of people have helped to make *Learning from Thoreau* possible. I'd especially like to thank Heloise Abtahi, Simon Baker, Doug Carlson, Stephen Corey, Bob Fogarty, Adam Gaynor, Elyse Goldberg, Bob Graham, the late Nancy Holt, John Kucich, Lucy Lippard, Scott Lucas, Connie Manoli-Skocay, Tom Martinelli, Amy Oppenheim, Lynn Rhoads, Julie Schilder, Beth Snead, Laura Walls, Ron Weaver, and Renee Williams. However, the person I owe the most to is my wife, Ruth Rachlin. Aside from her day-to-day support, we have shared many of the experiences recounted in the book, and my view of Thoreau often bears the imprint of our mutual response.

Because some of the chapters or passages in *Learning from Thoreau* appeared elsewhere in an earlier, often different form, I'd also like to thank the following journals and literary reviews for granting me permission to reprint this material:

"Blind Spot," *Georgia Review* 70, no. 1 (Spring 2016): 69–81. Copyright © 2017 by the University of Georgia.

"Nationalism and the Nature of Thoreau's 'Walking,'" *New England Quarterly* 85, no. 4 (December 2012): 591–621. Copyright © 2012 by MIT Press.

"Robert Smithson's Environmental History," *Oxford Art Journal* 37, no. 3 (2014): 285–304. Copyright © 2014 by Oxford University Press.

"Robert Smithson's Toxic Tour of Passaic, New Jersey," *Journal of American Studies* 48, no 4 (2014): 1019–40. Copyright © 2014 by Cambridge University Press.

"The Aesthetic Imperatives of Thoreau's 'Autumnal Tints,'" *ESQ: A Journal of the American Renaissance* 61, no. 4 (Fall 2015): 565–99. Copyright © 2015 by the Board of Regents of Washington State University.

"Cutting Edge," *Antioch Review* 75, no. 3 (Summer 2017): 301–12. Copyright © 2017 by Andrew Menard.

NOTES

Introduction

2   *"This winter they are cutting"*   Thoreau, *Journal*, ed. Torrey and Allen, January 21, 1852, 3:212–13.

3   *"I usually go to the village"*   Thoreau, *Walden*, 414.

3   *"community bathtub"*   Quoted in Leslie Perrin Wilson, 664.

3   *"He made the whole world"*   Burroughs, 375.

4   *"counter friction"*   Thoreau, *Collected Essays*, 211.

4   *"more perfect and glorious State"*   Ibid., 224.

5   *"I wish to speak"*   Ibid., 225.

7   *"have a kind of picture book"*   Smithson, 230.

8   *"there is no going back"*; *"wishy-washy transcendentalism"*   Ibid., 237, 163.

8   *"We used to renew"*   Koolhaas, n.p.

8   *"It is in vain"*   Thoreau, *Journal*, ed. Torrey and Allen, August 30, 1856, 9:43.

8   *"arranging what we have always known"*   Wittgenstein, 47.

9   *"watchman"*   Cavell, 40.

9   *"The earth is not"*   Thoreau, *Walden*, 568.

Chapter 1. Concord

10   *"Young men were born"*   Quoted in Kateb, *Emerson*, 43.

10   *Evidently, he was about five feet, seven inches tall*   Except where noted below, all biographical facts have been compiled from Harding, 124, 139, 237–38, 255, 264, 273, 295, 309, 319, 346, 353–54, 380, 415, and Sims, 11, 18, 34, 75, 157–58, 222. Laura Dassow Walls's new biography, *A Life*, wasn't available as I was writing the book.

10   *"features were quite marked"*   Channing, 33.

11   *"ugly as sin"*   Quoted in Petrulionis, 28.

11   *"eyes seldom left the ground"*   Ibid., 57.

11   *"dithyrambic dances"*   Ibid., 48.

11   *"His senses were acute"*   Emerson, "Thoreau," 242.

11   *recounted in Walter Harding's*   Harding, 55.

12   *"Cleave to the simplest"*   Thoreau, *Correspondence*, 386.

12   *"I have a real genius"*   Ibid., 369.

12   *"as adventurous as Crusoe's"*   Thoreau, *Journal 1, 1837–1844*, November 9, 1840, 196.

12   *"reverence for home"*   Blakemore, 115.

12   *the usual psychological probing*   See, for instance, both Lebeaux and Bridgman.

12   *"born talker"; "born reformer"*   Harding, 10, 9.

13   *but not very useful*   An exception is Arsić, who directly links Thoreau's grief about John to a sense of nature and place.

13   *"catholic virgin mother"*   Quoted in Harding, 111.

14   *"negative superiorities"*   Stevenson, 665.

14   *"in his presence"*   Quoted in Petrulionis, 32.

14   *"it was like the reproof"*   Ibid., 79.

14   *Even those who admired Thoreau*   There has always been a debate about the "good" Thoreau versus the "bad" Thoreau—explicitly summed up in the brief essay by George Willis Cooke that begins, "There are evidently two Thoreaus—one that of his admirers, and the other that of his detractors." For a recent example of the debate, see Kathryn Schulz's version of the "bad" Thoreau, followed by Donovan Hohn's rejoinder to Schulz.

14   *"He was a born protestant"*   Emerson, "Thoreau," 239.

14   *"few lives contain"; "as if he did not feel himself"*   Ibid., 240.

14   *"a fallacy to expose"*   Ibid.

14   *"couldn't put his life"*   Quoted in Petrulionis, 111.

15   *"be truly polar with humanity"*   Stevenson, 665.

15   *"Those who have most loudly"*   Lowell, 605.

15   *"In any circumstance"*   Emerson, "Thoreau," 241.

16   *"I have never got over"*   Thoreau, *Journal*, ed. Torrey and Allen, December 5, 1856, 9:160.

16   *"Take the shortest way"*   Ibid., November 1, 1858, 11:275.

17   *"the strongest natures"*   Woolf, 134.

17   *"I have been looking"*   Quoted in Harding, 12.

17   *"My desire is to know"*   Thoreau, *Journal*, ed. Torrey and Allen, November 12, 1837, 1:9.

17   *"Every man is tasked"*   Thoreau, *Walden*, 354.

18   *I'd cite the time*   My father heard this story from a colleague at Caltech and passed it along to me.

18   *"coming into this particular body"* Plotinus, 91.
18   *"every man is a warrior"* Thoreau, *Journal*, ed. Torrey and Allen,
      May 14, 1840, 1:135.
18   *"the noble life is continuous"* Ibid., August 23, 1845, 1:385.
18   *"my genius dates"* Thoreau, *A Week*, 45.
18   *"I don't want to feel"* Thoreau, *Journal*, ed. Torrey and Allen,
      December 25, 1841, 1:299.
18   *"Here I am"* Ibid., July 18, 1851, 2:316.
19   *"Little is to be expected"* Thoreau, *Walden*, 393.
19   *"I don't think that there's a stable"*; *"That can mean
      adopting"* Goldsmith, 83, 84.
19   *"unoriginal genius"* Quoted in Goldsmith, 1.
19   *"no matter where"* Channing, 38.
21   *"The ancient precept"* Emerson, *Essays*, 56.
22   *"I feel that I draw nearest"* Thoreau, *Journal 2, 1842–1848*, October 30,
      1842, 55.
22   *"I will wait the breezes"* Thoreau, *Journal*, ed. Torrey and Allen, March
      11, 1842, 1:326.
22   *"The morning must remind"* Thoreau, *Journal 2, 1842–1848*, April 18,
      1846, 235.
22   *"was one of those"* Channing, 12.
22   *"In youth before I lost"* Thoreau, *Journal*, ed. Torrey and Allen, July 16,
      1851, 2:306–7.
23   *"I think that no experience"* Ibid., July 16, 1851, 2:306.
23   *"Twenty-three years since"* Ibid., August 6, 1845, 1:380–81.
23   *"an original relation"* Emerson, *Essays*, 7.
23   *"point d'appui"* Thoreau, *Walden*, 400.
23–24 *"hard bottom and rocks in place"* Ibid.
24   *"I think I could write"* Thoreau, *Journal*, ed. Torrey and Allen,
      September 4, 1841, 1:282.
24   *house-tree-person test* A way of picturing, and thus interpreting,
      someone's inner world through simple images of home, nature,
      and self.
24   *"total object"* Beckett, 101.
24   *"Be native to the universe"* Thoreau, *Journal*, ed. Torrey and Allen, July
      16, 1850, 2:46.
25   *"deserved well of Mapledom"* Thoreau, *Collected Essays*, 375.
25   *"How much, what infinite"* Thoreau, *Journal*, ed. Torrey and Allen,
      December 28, 1852, 4:433–34.
25   *"Nature must be viewed"* Ibid., June 30, 1852, 4:163.
25   *"of extolling his own town"* Emerson, "Thoreau," 244.

Chapter 2. Walden

26   *"I lived alone"*   Thoreau, *Walden*, 325.

26   *"wooden inkstand"*   Channing, 230.

27   *"The complete subjugation"*   Thoreau, *Journal*, ed. Torrey and Allen, 1837–47, 1:487.

28   *"In the true natural order"*   Ibid., October 13, 1860, 14:119.

28   *"emotion recollected in tranquility"*   Wordsworth, 21.

28   *"I succeed best"*   Thoreau, *Journal*, ed. Torrey and Allen, May 5, 1852, 4:20.

29   *"What an immeasurable interval"*   Ibid., July 6, 1851, 2:284.

29   *"It is wonderful"*   Ibid., July 6, 1851, 2:284.

29   *"There are some intervals"*   Thoreau, *Collected Essays*, 240.

29   *"It bursts up"*   Ibid., 346.

30   *"did not belong to him"*   Ozick, 49.

31   *"prone to sing"*   Thoreau, *Early Essays*, 41.

31   *"away from himself"*   Emerson, *Essays*, 278.

32   *"different intention of the eye"*   Thoreau, *Collected Essays*, 394.

32   *"We cannot see anything"*   Ibid., 393.

33   *"What is most striking"*   Thoreau, *Maine Woods*, 652.

33   *"something savage and awful"*   Ibid., 645.

33   *"What is nature unless"*   Thoreau, *Journal*, ed. Torrey and Allen, November 2, 1853, 5:472.

34   *"It was a relief"*   Thoreau, *Maine Woods*, 711.

35   *"How much, what infinite"*   Thoreau, *Journal*, ed. Torrey and Allen, December 28, 1852, 4:433–34.

35   *"I am interested in each contemporary plant"*   Ibid., June 5, 1857, 9:406.

35   *"I can hardly believe"*   Ibid., September 12, 1851, 2:498.

36   *"Why should I hear"*   Ibid., April 18, 1852, 3:438.

36   *"Here I have been"*   Ibid., November 20, 1857, 10:191.

36   *"Why, the roots of letters"*   Ibid., October 16, 1859, 12:389.

37   *"Men nowhere, east or west"*   Thoreau, *A Week*, 307.

37   *"is a fixed point"*   Emerson, *Essays*, 42.

38   *"With the knowledge"*   Thoreau, *Journal*, ed. Torrey and Allen, August 29, 1858, 11:137.

39   *"From the beginning until now"*   Stein, 140.

39   *"There is no proposition"*   Borges, 171.

40   *"of the Unseen"*   Alcott, 444.

40   *"I wonder if"*   Carroll, 17.

41   *"full margin"*   Quoted in Sontag, 12.

41   *"double a deformity"*   Thoreau, *Journal*, ed. Torrey and Allen, February 14, 1840, 1:119.

Chapter 3. Walking

42   *"sauntering," "beautifully derived," etc.*   Thoreau, *Collected Essays*, 225–26.

43   *"Under his arm"*   Emerson, "Thoreau," 244.

43   *"between west and south-southwest"*   Thoreau, *Collected Essays*, 234.

43   *"Go to the Deep Cut," etc.*   Thoreau, *Journal*, ed. Torrey and Allen, December 30, 1851, 3:161, November 12, 1851, 3:110, September 29, 1851, 3:34, October 15, 1851, 3:72.

43   *"experiment"*   Latour, *Politics of Nature*, 195–96.

44   *"Sometimes, where the matter was"*   Channing, 10.

44   *"in my walks"*   Thoreau, *Collected Essays*, 229.

44   *"Let us then suppose"*   Locke, II:1:2–4, 121–23.

44   *"unimpaired senses"*   Quoted in Bowen, 45.

44–45   *"God has not been so sparing"*   Locke, IV:17:4, 391.

45   *"We need pray"*   Thoreau, *A Week*, 310.

45   *"What a faculty must that be"*   Thoreau, *Journal*, ed. Torrey and Allen, August 21, 1851, 2:413.

45   *"We live in a world of languages"*   Milosz and Gardels, n.p.

45   *"Every new flower"*   Thoreau, *Journal*, ed. Torrey and Allen, May 23, 1853, 5:184.

46   *"The true man of science"*   Thoreau, *Collected Essays*, 41.

47   *gait of finitude*   Solnit includes a brief but informative discussion of Kierkegaard's philosophical approach to walking, 23–26; she also has some interesting things to say about Wordsworth, as well as the Situationist theory of the "derive," or drift, that arose in the 1950s.

47   *"We want to walk"*   Wittgenstein, 46.

47   *"astonished at the power"*   Thoreau, *Collected Essays*, 227.

48   *"I remember gazing"*   Thoreau, *Journal*, ed. Torrey and Allen, December 4, 1856, 9:157.

48   *"the duration and extent"*   Virilio, 62.

48   *"I wish I had a heart"*   Keats, 30.

48   *"Nature has looked"*   Thoreau, *Journal*, ed. Torrey and Allen, June 21, 1852, 4:126.

49   *"the truth of a phenomenon"*   Virilio, 23.

49   *"And here, on the top"*   Thoreau, *Collected Essays*, 46.

50   *"I wonder that I ever"*   Thoreau, *Journal*, ed. Torrey and Allen, June 7, 1851, 2:228–29.

50   *"never took us"*   Quoted in Petrulionis, 44.

50   *"dos and don'ts"*   Lefebvre, 142.

50   *"The aspects of "*   Thoreau, *Journal*, ed. Torrey and Allen, May 23, 1841, 1:260.

50   *"How differently the poet"* Ibid., September 9, 1858, 11:153.

50   *"If you would make acquaintance"* Ibid., October 4, 1859, 12:371.

51   *"I fear that the character"* Ibid., August 19, 1851, 2:406.

51   *"Let us remember"* Ibid., June 20, 1840, 1:146.

52   *"distinctions too limited"* Paine, 23, 20.

52   *"self-reliance is precisely"* Emerson, *Complete Works*, 390.

52   *"most of the circumstances"* Griswold, 15.

52   *a report that the explorer John Frémont* For an analysis of how Frémont developed this aesthetic, see Menard, *Sight Unseen*, 41–43, 70–71.

53   *"reminds the traveller," etc.* Thoreau, *Collected Essays*, 44–51.

53   *"Before I walked"* Thoreau, *Journal*, ed. Torrey and Allen, January 7, 1851, 2:139.

53   *"What you call barrenness"* Ibid., December 5, 1856, 9:160.

53   *"I have been surprised"* Ibid., 1850, 2:13.

53   *"I had no idea"* Ibid., 1850, 2:15.

53   *"English literature, from the days"* Thoreau, *Collected Essays*, 244.

54   *"Walk often in drizzly weather"* Thoreau, *Journal*, ed. Torrey and Allen, September 3, 1851, 2:451.

54   *"the thing itself"* Thoreau, *Cape Cod*, 893.

55   *"only a musquash"* Thoreau, *Collected Essays*, 255.

55   *"nothing out of the ordinary"* Wittgenstein, 44.

56   *"lives extempore"* Quoted in Guthrie, 238.

56   *"one of the innate tendencies"* North, 61, 124.

56   *"all things are in revolution"* Thoreau, *Journal 2, 1842–1848*, after August 1, 1844, 102.

56   *"By the mediation"* Thoreau, *Journal*, ed. Torrey and Allen, March 13, 1842, 1:328.

Chapter 4. Seeing

59   *"The philosopher for whom"* Thoreau, *Journal*, ed. Torrey and Allen, November 5, 1857, 10:164–65.

60   *"Yes, but not necessarily"* Quoted in Sterritt, 20.

60–61 *"a fight against the fascination"* The phrase is from notes taken during Wittgenstein's lectures and later published as *The Blue and Brown Books*. Quoted in McGinn, 12.

62   *"the dog at three fourteen"* Borges, 65.

62   *"I have found"* Thoreau, *Collected Essays*, 394.

62   *"We notice that"* Thoreau, *A Week*, 40.

63   *"No one but a botanist"*   Thoreau, *Journal*, ed. Torrey and Allen, August 1, 1860, 14:3.

63   *"seeing"; "seeing-as"*   All quotes in the next few pages from Wittgenstein, 194–97.

64   *"There can be no peace"*   Noth seems to be fascinated by gestalts. A more recent cartoon in the *New Yorker* shows the "wife/mother-in-law" figure using a table lamp and her hands to project a shadow-image of the duck-rabbit onto the wall of a child's bedroom.

65   *"Such doubleness and distance"*   Thoreau, *Journal*, ed. Torrey and Allen, November 1, 1858, 11:273.

65   *"reconciliation of opposites"*   Coleridge, 150.

66   *"where they do not say 'moon'"*   Borges, 9.

66   *"Innumerable little streams"*   Thoreau, *Walden*, 565.

66   *"Walden is blue at one time"*   Ibid., 463.

67   *"Stand under this tree"*   Thoreau, *Collected Essays*, 387–88.

67   *"Scared up three blue herons"*   Thoreau, *Journal*, ed. Torrey and Allen, April 19, 1852, 3:443–44.

68   *"The question is not"*   Ibid., August 6, 1851, 2:373.

68   *"I am interested in an indistinct prospect"*   Ibid., July 29, 1857, 9:495.

68   *"A philosophical problem"; "You approach from one side"; "The aspects of things"*   Wittgenstein, 123, 82, 50.

69   *"What shall we make of the fact"*   Thoreau, *Journal*, ed. Torrey and Allen, 1850, 2:51.

69   *"the new can be not some object"*   Quoted in North, 160.

69   *"who describes the most familiar object"*   Thoreau, *Journal*, ed. Torrey and Allen, October 13, 1860, 14:120.

69   *"objects are concealed from"*   Thoreau, *Collected Essays*, 393.

69   *"If I invert my head"*   Thoreau, *Journal*, ed. Torrey and Allen, February 9, 1852, 3:291.

69   *"Plain speech is always"*   Thoreau, *Ibid.*, March 23, 1842, 1:342.

70   *Peck's exemplary list*   Peck, "Thoreau's Lakes," 95. Of the many studies written about Thoreau in recent decades, some of them now "classics," the ones I've found most helpful have been Bennett, *Thoreau's Nature*; Buell; Cavell; Garber; McIntosh; Peck, *Thoreau's Morning Work*; Richardson; and Walls, *Seeing New Worlds*.

70   *"nature will be my language"*   Thoreau, *Journal*, ed. Torrey and Allen, May 10, 1853, 5:135.

70   *"the sun or the earth"*   Schopenhauer, 23.

71   *"Is it not as language"*   Thoreau, *Journal*, ed. Torrey and Allen, August 7, 1853, 5: 359.

71	*"Let your walks"* Thoreau, *Collected Essays*, 393.
71	*"Ah, yes, here is the fall"* Fuller, 4–9.
72	*"strictly true to pictorial Nature"* Quoted in Wilkins, 69.
73	*"The main purpose"* "Inspiration Point," accessed 9 October 2017, www.yosemitehikes.com/yosemite-valley/inspiration-point/inspiration-point.htm.
74	*"most people who don't look too hard"* Smithson, 298.
74	*"we are as much as we see"* Thoreau, *Journal*, ed. Torrey and Allen, April 10, 1841, 1:248.

Chapter 5. Nature

75	*"Amonge these trees is fownde"* Quoted in Parrish, 25.
76	*"a sylvan soul"*; *"a genius of the natural world"* Quoted in Petrulionis, 7.
76	*"Nature, in return for his love"* Ibid., 28.
76	*"would have been competent"* Emerson, "Thoreau," 242.
76	*"most wrong upon his points of pride"*; *"Even when he says"* Eckstorm, 244, 245.
76	*"gauged everything by his beloved Concord River"* Quoted in Petrulionis, 178.
76	*"up and out at all hours"* Burroughs, 377, 378.
77	*"never intended to add"* Angelo, xliii.
77	*"remarkably acute ecological insights"*; *"issues in plant population"* Nabhan, xiv.
77	*"no more than a couple hundred yards"* Ibid., xv.
77	*"I omit the unusual"* Thoreau, *Journal*, ed. Torrey and Allen, August 28, 1851, 2:428.
77	*"The golden mean"* Ibid., July 8, 1840, 1:163–64.
77	*"the line of greatest length"* Thoreau, *Walden*, 552–53.
78	*"What I have observed"* Ibid., 554.
78	*"the most natural system"* Thoreau, *Journal*, ed. Torrey and Allen, December 4, 1856, 9:157.
78	*Kalendar* For a fine discussion of the Kalendar and a reproduction of the November entry, see Peck, *Thoreau's Morning Work*, 163–68.
78–79	*a kind of environmental golden mean* To understand what Concord was like during Thoreau's lifetime, I have benefitted from many of the essays in Schofield and Baron, especially part 6; also from both Foster and Thorson throughout.
79	*"if you took a handful"* Austin, 185–86.
79	*"endowed with intentionality"* Descola, 86.
80	*"May we not suspect"* Darwin, 288.

80   *the ecology of fear*   see Eisenberg.

80   *Darwin's emphasis on nature's balance*   For an analysis of how the idea of scarcity affected Thoreau, contributing to his love of the average, see Birch and Metting.

81   *"object is faithfully to describe"*   Thoreau, *Journal*, ed. Torrey and Allen, December 8, 1837, 1:15.

81   *"While walking in the Public gardens"*   Goethe, 366.

81   *"It struck me"*   Thoreau, *Collected Essays*, 38.

82   *"some one has said"*   Thoreau, *Journal 2, 1842–1848*, 80.

82   *"a truly grotesque vegetation"*   Thoreau, *Walden*, 565.

82   *"the eye rests"*   Thoreau, *Collected Essays*, 388.

82   *as historian Philip Rehbock has shown*   Rehbock, 7–10.

82   *"I was struck by"*   Thoreau, *Journal*, ed. Torrey and Allen, November 5, 1860, 14:218.

83   *"There is no French revolution"*   Ibid., June 11, 1851, 2:239.

83   *"By a beautiful law"*   Ibid., April 22, 1859, 12:155.

84   *"the year has many seasons more"*   Ibid., 1850, 2:21.

84   *"ontological properties"*   Descola, 99.

84   *"I remember gazing"*   Thoreau, *Journal*, ed. Torrey and Allen, December 4, 1856, 9:157.

85   *"first, the thin woody"*   Ibid., November 23, 1857, 10:196.

85   *"the filling up of a swamp"*   Ibid., February 1, 1858, 10:270.

87   *"the red squirrel"*   Ibid., March 10, 1855, 7:238.

88   *"He who cuts down woods"*   Ibid., May 17, 1853, 5:169.

88   *"putting forth two short twigs," etc.*   Thoreau, *Collected Essays*, 454–55.

88   *"I soon found myself"*   Thoreau, *Journal*, ed. Torrey and Allen, December 4, 1856, 9:158.

89   *"The whole North American forest"*   Ibid., May 16, 1860, 13:295–96.

89   *"the father of," floating down the Assabet*   Thoreau, *Journal*, ed. Torrey and Allen, July 2, 1853, 5:309–10, August 18, 1856, 9:8–9.

89   *"airborne vapor"*   Wilson, *Meaning*, 89.

90   *"not known even to"*   Ibid., 124; all subsequent facts and figures in paragraph from Edward O. Wilson, *Future*, 14–15.

90   *Even now it's hard to believe*   All three of these clonal colonies, as they're called, are beautifully described and pictured in Sussman.

90   *"it couldn't be any plainer"*   Dawkins, *Blind*, 111.

91   *"self-replicating biology"*   Venter, 129.

91   *"all the books"; "it suffices that a book"*   Borges, 54, 57.

91   *"I plan to compose my own text"*   Bök, "Xenotext Experiment," 229.

91   *"the average environment of the species"*   Dawkins, *River*, 29.

92   *"an elaborate code-script"*   Schrödinger, 61.

92   *"your term 'aperiodic crystal'"*   Quoted in Venter, 5.

92   *"a secure position"*   Edward O. Wilson, *Future*, 135.

93   *"sweet edge," "through the heart and marrow"*   Thoreau, *Walden*, 400.

93   *"More than any other botanist of his time"*   Nabhan, xvi.

93   *"Here I have been"*   Thoreau, *Journal*, ed. Torrey and Allen, November 20, 1857, 10:191.

Chapter 6. Wildness

95   *"man-made geological networks"*   Smithson, 8.

96   *"Niagara looks like a giant open pit quarry"*   Ibid., 308.

96   *"would rather retreat to scenic beauty spots"*   Ibid., 164.

96   *"A kind of 'virgin' beauty"*   Ibid., 298.

96   *"there is no going back to Paradise"*   Ibid., 237.

97   *"different types of sameness"*   Ibid., 115.

97   *"YOUR HIGHWAY TAXES 21 AT WORK"*   Ibid., 71.

97   *"woodsy witchdoctors"*   Quoted in Nash, 240.

97   *"the grim facts"; "Wherever we look"*   Rosenblum, 35, 37.

98   *"wishy-washy transcendentalism"*   Smithson, 163.

98   *"pavements, holes, trenches"*   Ibid., 95.

98   *The early colonists*   See Hall, 1–16.

98   *Genesis 1:28*   Cotton, 6.

99   *"use, but don't waste"*   Cooper, 237.

99   *"community of perills"*   Winthrop, 192.

99   *"Mickey Mouse"*   Smithson, 230.

99   *"It strikes the European traveller"*   Willis, 1:1.

100   *"iron tramp"*   Cole, 100–109.

100   *"her wilderness will be"*   Quoted in Brogan, 138.

100   *"the most alive is the wildest"*   Thoreau, *Collected Essays*, 240.

100   *"It is the bog in our brain"*   Thoreau, *Journal*, ed. Torrey and Allen, August 30, 1856, 9:43.

100   *"substituting for the obvious word"*   Emerson, "Thoreau," 247.

101   *"behind each little pebble"*   Thoreau, *Journal*, ed. Torrey and Allen, November 3, 1861, 14:346.

101   *"fuzzy empire of blur"*   Koolhaas, n.p.

101   *"one well-conducted institution"*   Thoreau, *Walden*, 416.

101   *"this one hillside"*   Ibid., 568.

102   *"I imagine it to be"*   Thoreau, *Journal*, ed. Torrey and Allen, July 14, 1845, 1:367.

102   *"By the twentieth of August," etc.*   Thoreau, *Collected Essays*, 369–70.

103   *dollies in like a movie camera*   For an interesting, though in my view overstated, account of Thoreau's relation to photography as a medium and a way of seeing, see Meehan.

104   *"the sublime melting into"*   Cole, 103.

104   *"The clearest way"*   Muir, 312.

104   *"I am interested in each contemporary plant"*   Thoreau, *Journal*, ed. Torrey and Allen, June 5, 1857, 9:406.

105   *"geologic agent"*   Smithson, 298.

105   *"The civilized nations"*   Thoreau, *Collected Essays*, 243.

105   *"wild, rank, luxuriant place"*   Thoreau, *Journal*, ed. Torrey and Allen, November 14, 1850, 2:95.

105   *"I would not have every man"*   Thoreau, *Collected Essays*, 249.

105   *"the great harvest of the year"*   Ibid., 381.

105   *"interchangeable distances"*   Smithson, 254.

105   *"unfinished cities"*   Ibid., 101.

106   *"incalculable cycles"*   Ibid., 67.

106   *"jejune experiment"*   Ibid., 74.

107   *"It is wonderful," etc.*   Thoreau, *Walden*, 565–67.

108   *"we live in an emergent"*   Kauffman, 130.

108   *"the hidden, the improbable"*   Latour, "Will Non-Humans," 220.

108   *by what modern cartographers call "trap streets"*   For these and many other aspects of what's rather promiscuously called the New Aesthetic, see Bridle.

109   *"Standing on a mountain"*   Thoreau, *Maine Woods*, 727.

109   *"We live on the verge"*   Thoreau, *A Week*, 309.

109   *"All nature is in"*   Thoreau, *Journal*, ed. Torrey and Allen, June 14, 1851, 2:254–55.

109   *"I hear beyond the range"*   Thoreau, *Collected Essays*, 557.

109   *"Having by chance"*   Thoreau, *Journal*, ed. Torrey and Allen, January 22, 1852, 3:217.

109   *"My practicalness"*   Ibid., June 7, 1851, 2:228.

110   *"It is a certain faeryland"*   Ibid., June 7, 1851, 2:228.

110   *"We affirm that"*   Ibid., June 7, 1851, 2:229.

110   *"a ghost wilderness"*   Snyder, 22.

110   *"I have great faith"*   Thoreau, *Collected Essays*, 442.

110   *"The very earth itself"*   Thoreau, *Faith in a Seed*, 151.

110   *"defined by changes"*   Foster, 62.

110   *"There are idle spots"*   Leopold, 48.

111   *"unable to withstand"*   Bradshaw, 173.

111   *"horizon beyond"; "heaven above"*   Sloterdijk, 77.

112   *"all good things"* Thoreau, *Collected Essays,* 246.

112   *"in Wildness"* Ibid., 239.

Chapter 7. Beauty

114   *or so Alexander von Humboldt* Humboldt, *Cosmos,* 2:38.

114   *nature on its own terms* Kant, §§ 2, 16.

114   *"The era of the Wild Apple"* Thoreau, *Collected Essays,* 466.

114   *"What sort of country"* Ibid., 493.

114   *"To the New England mind"* Henry Adams, 49.

115   *"All our improvements"* Thoreau, *Collected Essays,* 495.

116   *close and sustained interest* Kant, § 42; *abstract set of rules:* § 59.

116   *"a medium intellectual state"* Thoreau, *Journal 1, 1837–1844,* September 28, 1843, 468.

116   *"deliberately cultivated sensibility"* Bennett, *Enchantment,* 29.

116   *"Objects are concealed"* Thoreau, *Collected Essays,* 393.

117   *objective beauty, persuasion* Kant, §§ 7–8, 18–19, 22, 32, 37–38.

117   *"Space and time"* Gabo and Pevsner, 9.

117   *"appropriateness"* Kant, §§ 14–16.

117   *"It has faithfully discharged"* Thoreau, *Collected Essays,* 375.

117   *"It is remarkable"* Thoreau, *Journal,* ed. Torrey and Allen, March 7, 1854, 6:156.

117   *"The pincushion galls"* Ibid., June 1, 1853, 5:210.

118   *had to be regulated* Dewey, 12.

119   *"What are the natural features"* Thoreau, *Collected Essays,* 496.

119   *"Saving does not only"* Heidegger, 352.

120   *"It is the will of the Nation"* Olmsted, 500.

120   *"the enjoyment of"* Ibid., 504.

120   *"great public grounds"* Ibid., 505.

120   *"It is in no scene"* Ibid., 500.

120   *"the difference in the elevation"* Ibid., 493.

121   *"the value of the district"* Ibid., 506.

121   *"the millions who are hereafter," etc.* Ibid., 507–8.

121   *fully engineered landscape* For a discussion of Olmsted's fully engineered landscape, see Menard, "Enlarged Freedom."

121   *"Nature, this sacrosanct Nature"* Latour, "'It's Development, Stupid!'" 6.

121   *"Island Civilization"* Nash, 379–85.

123   *A river, Douglas claimed* Douglas, 743, 741–42, 745, 745–46, 749, 743.

124   *"There is a higher law"* Thoreau, *Maine Woods,* 684–85.

124   *"this generation has altered"* Johnson, 161.

125   *"the most important conservation law"* Edward O. Wilson, *Future,* 185.

125   *"innate tendency"*   Edward O. Wilson, *Biophilia*, 1.

125   *"innately emotional affiliation"*   Edward O. Wilson, "Biophilia and the Conservation Ethic," 31.

125   *"existential conservatism"*   Edward O. Wilson, *Meaning*, 60.

125   *"There is, no doubt"*   Thoreau, *Journal*, ed. Torrey and Allen, May 20, 1851, 2:201.

125   *"The mystery of"*   Ibid., March 7, 1859, 12:23.

125   *"I wish to speak"*   Thoreau, *Collected Essays*, 225.

126   *"simply be read"*   Jamieson, 76.

126   *congressional committee in 1965*   Ibid., 21.

126   *"short-circuited"*   Latour, *Politics of Nature*, 4.

126   *"nothing wrong with accepting evidence"*   Jamieson, 92.

127   *"How important is a constant"*   Thoreau, *Journal*, ed. Torrey and Allen, May 6, 1851, 2:193.

127   *"Men nowhere, east or west"*   Thoreau, *A Week*, 307.

128   *"Such is beauty ever"*   Thoreau, *Journal*, ed. Torrey and Allen, January 21, 1838, 1:26.

128   *"on a humble scale"*   Thoreau, *Walden*, 463.

128   *"Swampes and such Rubbish waest grounds"*   Anonymous, 184.

128   *"experience its own destruction"*   Benjamin, 242. For a more recent discussion of beauty's downside, see Kateb, "Aestheticism and Morality." For anyone who believes, as I do, that beauty ought to play a more central role in critical and environmental thought, Kateb's essay is a must-read. It's a useful counter friction to Elaine Scarry's *On Beauty and Being Just*, as well as a number of Martha Nussbaum's generally excellent works.

128   *"Back to the Pleistocene"*   For an influential response to this line of thinking, itself influenced by Thoreau's notion of wildness, see Cronon. For some examples of how European conservationists, lacking our mythology of wilderness and the frontier, have avoided this approach from the start, see both Hall and Kolbert.

129   *"of the finest conceivable"*   Thoreau, *Journal*, ed. Torrey and Allen, November 1, 1853, 5:469.

129   *"the pearls of Walden"*   Ibid., January 25, 1853, 4:476.

Conclusion

131   *"There's nothing there"*   Quoted in Taylor, 16.

131   *"I don't think art"*   De Maria, 630.

133   *"ecological despair"*; *"modern day ecologists"*; *"the operations of industry"*; *"image of the lost paradise garden"*   Smithson, 161.

133   *"It reminds me of"*   Ibid., 158.

134   *Lippard admits*   Lippard, 88, 82.

134   *middle-sized objects*   Jamieson, 4.

135   *"Few phenomena"*   This and all subsequent quotes related to the melting sands of the Deep Cut in Thoreau, *Walden*, 565–68.

138   *"Regarded as water"*   Thoreau, *Collected Essays*, 388–89.

139   *"The drops grow"*   Haacke, 6.

140   *A decade later, Mel Chin*   Chin, 174–75.

140   *number of vibrant "paintings"*   Warn, n.p.

140   *"agar-covered acrylic plates"*   Gessert, 66.

140   *"The engineered apple"*   House, online, n.p.

141   *"a word is a bit of crystal"*   Bök, *Crystallography*, 12.

141   *"I bitch; I kibbitz"*   Bök, *Eunoia*, 50.

142   *"trying to write a book of poetry"*   Bök, "Christian Bök: Interview," 60.

142   *"poetic cypher, gene X-P13"*   Bök, "Xenotext Works." n.p.

143   *"What Great Comet"*   Bök, *Xenotext: Book 1*, 15.

143   *"Why take pains"*   Wordsworth, 23.

144   *"not a wilderness"*   Quoted in Descola, 35–36.

BIBLIOGRAPHY

Adams, Henry. *The Education of Henry Adams.* New York: Penguin Books, 1995.

Adams, Robert. *The New West: Landscapes along the Colorado Front Range.* New York: Aperture, 2008.

Alcott, Bronson. "The Forester." *Atlantic Monthly* 9, no. 54 (April 1862): 443–46.

Alÿs, Francis. "When Faith Moves Mountains." Video, 15:09. Filmed 2004 in collaboration with Cuauhtémoc Medina and Rafael Ortega. http://www.francisalys/when-faith-moves-mountains. Published on companion DVD in Francis Alÿs et al., *When Faith Moves Mountains/Cuando la fe mueve montañas* (Madrid: Turner, 2005).

Angelo, Ray. "Thoreau as Botanist." In *Thoreau's Wildflowers*, edited by Geoff Wisner, xxvii–xliii. New Haven, Conn.: Yale University Press, 2016.

Anonymous. "Essay on the Ordering of Towns." In *Winthrop Papers*, vol. 3, *1631–1637*, 181–85. Boston: Massachusetts Historical Society, 1943.

Arsić, Branka. *Bird Relics: Grief and Vitalism in Thoreau.* Cambridge, Mass.: Harvard University Press, 2016.

Austin, Mary. *Earth Horizon: An Autobiography.* Albuquerque: University of New Mexico Press, 1991. Originally published 1932.

Beckett, Samuel. *Proust, and Three Dialogues with Georges Duthuit.* London: Calder and Boyars, 1965.

Benjamin, Walter. "The Work of Art in the Age of Mechanical Reproduction." In *Illuminations*, edited by Hannah Arendt, translated by Harry Zohn, 217–51. New York: Schocken Books, 1969.

Bennett, Jane. *The Enchantment of Modern Life: Attachments, Crossings, and Ethics.* Princeton, N.J.: Princeton University Press, 2001.

———. *Thoreau's Nature: Ethics, Politics, and the Wild.* Lanham, Md.: Rowman and Littlefield, 1994.

Birch, Thomas D., and Fred Metting. "The Economic Design of *Walden*." *New England Quarterly* 65, no. 4 (December 1992): 587–602.

Blakemore, Peter. "Reading Home: Thoreau, Literature, and the Phenomenon of Inhabitation." In *Thoreau's Sense of Place: Essays in American Environmental*

Writing, edited by Richard J. Schneider, 115–32. Iowa City: University of Iowa Press, 2000.

Bök, Christian. "Christian Bök: Interview by Jonathan Ball." *Believer* 7, no. 5 (June 2009): 59–66.

———. *Crystallography*. Ontario, Canada: Coach House Books, 2003.

———. *Eunoia*. Ontario, Canada: Coach House Books, 2005.

———. *The Xenotext: Book 1*. Ontario, Canada: Coach House Books, 2015.

———. "The Xenotext Experiment." *SCRIPTed* 5, no. 2 (August 2008), 227–31.

———. "The Xenotext Works." *Harriett* (blog), Poetry Foundation, April 2nd, 2011. http://www.poetryfoundation.org/harriet/2011/04/the-xenotext-works.

Borges, Jorge Luis. *Labyrinths: Selected Stories and Other Writings*. New York: New Directions, 1964.

Bowen, Margarita. *Empiricism and Geographical Thought: From Francis Bacon to Alexander von Humboldt*. New York: Cambridge University Press, 1981.

Bradshaw, Anthony D. "Alternative Endpoints for Reclamation." In *Rehabilitating Damaged Ecosystems*, edited by John Cairns Jr., 165–86. Boca Raton, Fla.: CRC Press, 1995.

Bridgman, Richard. *Dark Thoreau*. Lincoln: University of Nebraska Press, 1982.

Bridle, James. "Waving at the Machines." Video and transcript of keynote address given at Web Directions South 2011, October 14, 2011, Sydney, Australia. http://www.webdirections.org/resources/james-bridle-waving -at-the-machines/.

Brogan, Hugh. *Alexis de Tocqueville: A Biography*. London: Profile Books, 2006.

Brückner, Martin. *The Geographic Revolution in Early America: Maps, Literacy, and National Identity*. Chapel Hill, N.C.: Published for the Omohundo Institute of Early American History and Culture by the University of North Carolina Press, 2006.

Buell, Lawrence. *The Environmental Imagination: Thoreau, Nature Writing, and the Formation of American Culture*. Cambridge, Mass.: Belknap Press of Harvard University Press, 1995.

Burroughs, John. "Henry D. Thoreau." *Century* 24, no. 3 (July 1882): 368–79.

Carroll, Lewis. *The Annotated Alice*. Edited by Martin Gardner. New York: W. W. Norton, 2000.

Cavell, Stanley. *The Senses of Walden: An Expanded Edition*. San Francisco: North Point Press, 1981.

Channing, William Ellery. *Thoreau: The Poet-Naturalist*. Edited by F. B. Sanborn. Boston: Charles E. Goodspeed, 1902.

Chin, Mel. "Mel Chin in Conversation with Fareed Armaly and Uta Meta Bauer." In *Nature*, edited by Jeffrey Kastner, 174–76. Cambridge, Mass.: MIT Press, 2012.

Cole, Thomas. "Essay on American Scenery." In *American Art, 1700–1960: Sources and Documents*, edited by John W. McCoubrey, 98–110. Englewood Cliffs, N.J.: Prentice-Hall, 1965.

Coleridge, Samuel Taylor. *Biographia Literaria; or, Biographical Sketches of My Literary Life and Opinions; and Two Lay Sermons*. London: George Bell, 1884.

Cooke, George Willis. "The Two Thoreaus." *Independent* 48 (December 10, 1866): 1671–72.

Cooper, James Fenimore. *The Pioneers*. New York: New American Library, 1964.

Cotton, John. *God's Promise to His Plantations*. Old South Leaflets (General Series), vol. 3, no. 53. Boston: Directors of the Old South Work, Old South Meeting House, [1894]. First published London, 1630.

Cronon, William. "The Trouble with Wilderness; or, Getting Back to the Wrong Nature." In *Uncommon Ground: Rethinking the Human Place in Nature*, edited by William Cronon, 69–90. New York: W. W. Norton, 1995.

Darwin, Charles. "A Biographical Sketch of an Infant." *Mind: A Quarterly Review of Psychology and Philosophy* 2, no. 7 (July 1877): 285–94.

Dawkins, Richard. *River Out of Eden: A Darwinian View of Life*. New York: Basic Books, 1995.

———. *The Blind Watchmaker*. New York: W. W. Norton and Co., 1986.

De Maria, Walter. "On the Importance of Natural Disasters." In *Theories and Documents of Contemporary Art: A Sourcebook of Artists' Writings*, edited by Kristine Styles and Peter Selz, 630. Berkeley: University of California Press, 2012.

Descola, Philippe. *Beyond Nature and Culture*. Translated by Janet Lloyd. Chicago: University of Chicago Press, 2013.

Dewey, John. *The Public and Its Problems*. Athens: Ohio University Press, 1991.

Douglas, William O. "Dissent." Sierra Club v. Morton, 405 U.S. 727 (1972), 741–49. Available online at http://caselaw.findlaw.com/us-supreme-court/405/727.html.

Eckstorm, Fanny Hardy. "Thoreau's 'Maine Woods.'" *Atlantic Monthly* 102, no. 2 (August 1908): 242–50.

Eisenberg, Cristina. "Quantifying Wilderness: A Scientist's Lessons about Wolves and Wild Nature." In *The Rediscovery of the Wild*, edited by Peter H. Kahn Jr. and Patricia H. Hasbach, 1–25. Cambridge, Mass.: MIT Press, 2013.

Eldridge, Niles, and Stephen J. Gould. "Punctuated Equilibria: An Alternative to Phyletic Gradualism." In *Models in Paleobiology*, edited by T. J. M. Schopf, 82–115. San Francisco: Freeman, Cooper, 1972.

Emerson, Ralph Waldo. *Essays and Lectures*. Edited by Joel Porte. New York: Library of America, 1983.

———. *The Complete Works of Ralph Waldo Emerson*. Vol. 2, *Essays: 1st series*. Boston: Houghton, Mifflin, 1904.

———. "Thoreau." *Atlantic Monthly* 10, no. 58 (August 1862): 239–49.

Foster, David R. *Thoreau's Country: Journey through a Transformed Landscape*. Cambridge, Mass.: Harvard University Press, 1999.

Franzen, Jonathan. *Freedom*. New York: Farrar, Straus and Giroux, 2010.

Fuller, Margaret. *Summer on the Lakes, in 1843*. Urbana: University of Illinois Press, 1991.

Gabo, Naum, and Antoine Pevsner. "The Realistic Manifesto." In *The Tradition of Constructivism*, edited by Stephen Bann, 3–11. New York: Da Capo, 1990.

Garber, Frederick. *Thoreau's Redemptive Imagination*. New York: New York University Press, 1977.

Gessert, George. "A Brief History of Art Involving DNA." In *Nature*, edited by Jeffrey Kastner, 63–67. Cambridge, Mass.: MIT Press, 2012.

Goethe, Johann Wolfgang von. *Italian Journey: 1786–1788*. New York: Penguin Books, 1970.

Goldsmith, Kenneth. *Uncreative Writing: Managing Language in the Digital Age*. New York: Columbia University Press, 2011.

Griswold, Rufus Wilmot. "The Intellectual History, Condition and Prospects of the Country." In *The Prose Writers of America*, 13–52. Philadelphia: Carey and Hart, 1847.

Guthrie, James. *Above Time: Emerson's and Thoreau's Temporal Revolutions*. Columbia: University of Missouri Press, 2001.

Haacke, Hans. *The Condensation Cube*. Barcelona Museum of Contemporary Art. http://www.macba.cat/en/condensation-cube-1532.

Hall, Marcus. *Earth Repair: A Transatlantic History of Environmental Restoration*. Charlottesville: University of Virginia Press, 2005.

Harding, Walter. *The Days of Henry Thoreau*. New York: Dover Publications, 1982.

Heidegger, Martin. "Building Dwelling Thinking." In *Basic Writings*, 2nd rev. and exp. ed., edited by David Farrell Krell, 343–65. Translated by Albert Hofstadter. New York: Harper Collins, 1993.

Hohn, Donovan. "Everybody Hates Henry." *New Republic*, October 21, 2015. https://newrepublic.com/article/123162/everybody-hates-henry-david-thoreau.

House, Patrick. "Object of Interest: The Twice Forbidden Fruit." *New Yorker*, May 13, 2014. http://www.newyorker.com/tech/elements/object-of-interest-the-twice-forbidden-fruit.

Humboldt, Alexander von. *Cosmos: A Sketch of the Physical Description of the Universe*. 2 vols. Translated by E. C. Otté. Baltimore, Md.: Johns Hopkins University Press, 1997.

Jamieson, Dale. *Reason in a Dark Time: Why the Struggle against Climate Change Failed—And What It Means for Our Future*. New York: Oxford University Press, 2014.

Johnson, Lyndon Baines. "Special Message to the Congress on Conservation and Restoration of Natural Beauty, February 8, 1965." In *Public Papers of the Presidents of the United States: Lyndon B. Johnson, 1965*, vol. 1, 155–65. Washington, D.C.: Government Printing Office, 1966. Available online at http://www.lbjlibrary.net/collections/selected-speeches/1965/02-08-1965.html.

Kant, Immanuel. *Critique of the Power of Judgment*. Edited by Paul Guyer. Translated by Paul Guyer and Eric Matthews. New York: Cambridge University Press, 2000.

Kateb, George. "Aestheticism and Morality: Their Cooperation and Hostility." In *Patriotism and Other Mistakes*. 117–49. New Haven, Conn.: Yale University Press, 2006.

———. *Emerson and Self-Reliance*. Lanham, Md.: Rowman and Littlefield, 2002.

Kauffman, Stuart A. *Reinventing the Sacred: A New View of Science, Reason, and Religion*. New York: Basic Books, 2008.

Keats, John. "John Keats to Benjamin Bailey, 28–30 October 1817." In *Letters of John Keats*, edited by Robert Gittings, 28–32. New York: Oxford University Press, 1988.

Kolbert, Elizabeth. "Recall of the Wild." *New Yorker*, December 24 and 31, 2012, 50–60.

Komar, Vitaly, and Alexander Melamid. "Painting by Numbers: The Search for a People's Art: An interview with Alex Melamid." *Nation*, March 14, 1994, 334–48.

Koolhaas, Rem. "Junkspace." In *Project on the City II: The Harvard Guide to Shopping*, edited by Judy Chung Chuihua, Jeffrey Inaba, Rem Koolhaas, and Sze Tsung Leong, n.p. Köln: Taschen, 2001.

Latour, Bruno. "'It's Development, Stupid!' or: How to Modernize Modernization." http://www.bruno-latour.fr/sites/default/files/107-NORDHAUS&SCHELLENBERGER.pdf. Published in shortened version as "Love Your Monsters," in *Love Your Monsters: Postenvironmentalism and the Anthropocene*, edited by Michael Shellenberger and Ted Nordhaus, 17–25. Oakland, Calif.: Breakthrough Institute, 2011.

———. *Politics of Nature: How to Bring the Sciences into Democracy*. Translated by Catherine Porter. Cambridge, Mass.: Harvard University Press, 2004.

———. "Will Non-Humans Be Saved? An Argument in Ecotheology." In *Nature*, edited by Jeffrey Kastner, 211–23. Cambridge, Mass.: MIT Press, 2012.

Lebeaux, Richard. *Young Man Thoreau*. Amherst: University of Massachusetts Press, 1977.

Lefebvre, Henri. *The Production of Space*. Translated by Donald Nicholson-Smith. Malden, Mass.: Blackwell, 1991.

Leopold, Aldo. *A Sand County Almanac and Sketches Here and There*. New York: Oxford University Press, 1989.

Lippard, Lucy R. *Undermining: A Wild Ride through Land Use, Politics, and Art in the Changing West*. New York: New Press, 2014.

Locke, John. *An Essay concerning Human Understanding*. 2 vols. Edited by Alexander Campbell Fraser. New York: Dover, 1959.

Louv, Richard. *Last Child in the Woods: Saving Our Children from Nature-Deficit Disorder*. Chapel Hill, N.C.: Algonquin, 2008.

Lowell, James Russell. "Critical Notices: Henry D. Thoreau's *Letters to Various Persons*." *North American Review* 101, no. 209 (October 1865): 597–608.

McGinn, Marie. *Wittgenstein and the Philosophical Investigations*. New York: Routledge, 1997.

McIntosh, James. *Thoreau As Romantic Naturalist: His Shifting Stance toward Nature*. Ithaca, NY: Cornell University Press, 1974.

Meehan, Sean Ross. *Mediating American Autobiography: Photography in Emerson, Thoreau, Douglass, and Whitman*. Columbia: University of Missouri Press, 2008.

Menard, Andrew. *Sight Unseen: How Frémont's First Expedition Changed the American Landscape*. Lincoln: University of Nebraska Press, 2012.

———. "The Enlarged Freedom of Frederick Law Olmsted." *New England Quarterly* 83, no. 3 (September 2010): 508–38.

Milosz, Czeslaw, and Nathan Gardels. "At Century's End: Recovering a Reverence for *Being*." *Los Angeles Times*, July 25, 1999. http://http://articles .latimes.com/1999/jul/25/books/bk-59268.

Mitchell, Joseph. "Days in the Branch." *New Yorker*, December 1, 2014, 40–45.

Muir, John. "The Philosophy of John Muir." In *The Wilderness World of John Muir*, edited by Edwin Way Teales, 311–24. New York: Houghton Mifflin, 2001.

Nabhan, Gary Paul. "Foreword: Learning the Language of Fields and Forests." In Henry D. Thoreau, *Faith in a Seed: The Dispersion of Seeds and Other Late Natural History Writings*, edited by Bradley P. Dean, xi–xviii. Washington, D.C.: Island Press, 1993.

Nash, Roderick. *Wilderness and the American Mind*. 5th ed. New Haven, Conn.: Yale University Press, 2014.

North, Michael. *Novelty: A History of the New*. Chicago: University of Chicago Press, 2013.

Olmsted, Frederick Law. "Preliminary Report upon the Yosemite and Big Tree Grove." In *The California Frontier, 1863–1865*, vol. 5, *The Papers of Frederick*

Law Olmsted, edited by Victoria Post Ranney, 488–511. Baltimore, Md.: Johns Hopkins University Press, 1990.

Ozick, Cynthia. "The Impossibility of Being Kafka." In *Quarrel and Quandary: Essays*, 42–58. New York: Vintage, 2000.

Paine, Thomas. *Rights of Man, Common Sense, and Other Political Writings.* Edited by Mark Philp. New York: Oxford University Press, 1995.

Parrish, Susan Scott. *American Curiosity: Cultures of Natural History in the Colonial British Atlantic World.* Chapel Hill: University of North Carolina Press, 2006.

Peck, H. Daniel. "Thoreau's Lakes of Light: Modes of Representation and the Enactment of Philosophy in *Walden*." *Midwest Studies in Philosophy* 28, no. 1 (2004): 85–101.

———. *Thoreau's Morning Work: Memory and Perception in* A Week on the Concord and Merrimack Rivers, *the Journal, and* Walden. New Haven, Conn.: Yale University Press, 1990.

Petrulionis, Sandra Harbert, ed. *Thoreau in His Own Time: A Biographical Chronicle of His Life, Drawn from Recollections, Interviews, and Memoirs by Family, Friends, and Associates.* Iowa City: University of Iowa Press, 2012.

Plotinus. *Ennead, vol. 2.* Translated by A. H. Armstrong. Loeb Classical Library 441. Cambridge, Mass.: Harvard University Press, 1966.

Rehbock, Philip F. *The Philosophical Naturalists: Themes in Early Nineteenth-Century British Biology.* Madison: University of Wisconsin Press, 1983.

Richardson, Robert D. *Henry Thoreau: A Life of the Mind.* Berkeley: University of California Press, 1986.

Rosenblum, Robert. "The Primal American Scene." In *The Natural Paradise: Painting in America 1800–1950*, edited by Kynaston McShine, 13–38. New York: Museum of Modern Art, 1976.

Ruskin, John. *The Elements of Drawing.* Whitefish, Mont.: Kessinger, 2005.

Schofield, Edmund A., and Robert C. Baron, eds. *Thoreau's World and Ours: A Natural Legacy.* Golden, Colo.: North American Press, 1993.

Schopenhauer, Arthur. *The World as Will and Representation.* Vol. 1. Edited and translated by Judith Norman, Alistair Welchman, and Christopher Janaway. New York: Cambridge University Press, 2010.

Schrödinger, Erwin. *What Is Life? The Physical Aspect of the Living Cell.* Cambridge: Cambridge University Press, 1992.

Schulz, Kathryn. "Pond Scum." *New Yorker*, October 19, 2015, 40–44.

Sims, Michael. *The Adventures of Henry Thoreau: A Young Man's Unlikely Path to Walden Pond.* New York: Bloomsbury, 2014.

Sloterdijk, Peter. *In the World Interior of Capital: Towards a Philosophical Theory of Globalization.* Translated by Wieland Hoban. Cambridge, U.K.: Polity, 2013.

Slotkin, Richard. *Regeneration through Violence: The Mythology of the American Frontier, 1600–1860.* Middletown, Conn.: Wesleyan University Press, 1973.

Smithson, Robert. *Robert Smithson: The Collected Writings.* Edited by Jack Flam. Berkeley: University of California Press, 1966.

Snyder, Gary. "The Etiquette of Freedom." In *The Practice of the Wild: Essays by Gary Snyder,* 3–24. San Francisco: North Point, 1990.

Solnit, Rebecca. *Wanderlust: A History of Walking.* New York: Penguin, 2000.

Sontag, Susan. "The Aesthetics of Silence." In *Styles of Radical Will,* 3–34. New York: Farrar, Straus and Giroux, 1966.

Specq, François, Laura Dassow Walls, and Michael Granger, eds. *Thoreauvian Modernities: Transatlantic Conversations on an American Icon.* Athens: University of Georgia Press, 2013.

Stein, Gertrude. "Poetry and Grammar." In *Look at Me Now and Here I Am: Writings and Lectures 1909–43,* ed. Patricia Meyerowitz, 125–47. Harmondsworth, U.K.: Penguin, 1971.

Sterritt, David. *The Films of Jean-Luc Godard: Seeing the Invisible.* New York: Cambridge University Press, 1999.

Stevenson, Robert Louis. "Henry David Thoreau: His Character and Opinions." *Cornhill Magazine* 41 (June 1880): 665–82.

Sullivan, Robert. *The Thoreau You Don't Know: What the Prophet of Environmentalism Really Meant.* New York: Collins, 2009.

Sussman, Rachel. *The Oldest Living Things in the World.* Chicago: University of Chicago Press, 2014.

Taylor, Mark C. "Rend(er)ing." In Michael Heizer, *Michael Heizer: Double Negative,* 12–22. Los Angeles: Museum of Contemporary Art; New York: Rizzoli, 1992.

Thoreau, Henry David. *Cape Cod.* In *A Week on the Concord and Merrimack Rivers, Walden, The Maine Woods, Cape Cod.* New York: Library of America, 1985.

———. *Collected Essays and Poems.* Edited by Elizabeth Hall Witherell. New York: Library of America, 2001.

———. *The Correspondence of Henry David Thoreau.* Edited by Walter Harding and Carl Bode. New York: New York University Press, 1958.

———. *Early Essays and Miscellanies.* Edited by Joseph J. Moldenhauer and Edwin Moser. Princeton, N.J.: Princeton University Press, 1975.

———. *Faith in a Seed: The Dispersion of Seeds and Other Late Natural History Writings.* Edited by Bradley P. Dean. Washington, D.C.: Island Press, 1993.

———. *The Journal of Henry D. Thoreau.* Edited by Bradford Torrey and Francis H. Allen, 14 vols. New York: Dover Publications, 1962. First published 1906 by Houghton, Mifflin. Cited in notes as *Journal,* ed. Torrey and Allen.

———. *The Maine Woods.* In *A Week on the Concord and Merrimack Rivers, Walden, The Maine Woods, Cape Cod.* New York: Library of America, 1985.

———. *Walden; or, Life in the Woods.* In *A Week on the Concord and Merrimack Rivers, Walden, The Maine Woods, Cape Cod.* New York: Library of America, 1985.

———. *A Week on the Concord and Merrimack Rivers.* In *A Week on the Concord and Merrimack Rivers, Walden, The Maine Woods, Cape Cod.* New York: Library of America, 1985.

———. *Wild Fruits: Thoreau's Rediscovered Last Manuscript.* Edited by Bradley P. Dean. New York: W. W. Norton, 2000.

———. *The Writings of Henry D. Thoreau: Journal 1, 1837–1844.* Edited by Elizabeth Witherell, William L. Howarth, Robert Sattelmeyer, and Thomas Blanding. Princeton, N.J.: Princeton University Press, 1981. Cited in notes as *Journal 1, 1837–1844.*

———. *The Writings of Henry D. Thoreau: Journal 2, 1842–1848.* Edited by Robert Sattelmeyer. Princeton, N.J.: Princeton University Press, 1984. Cited in notes as *Journal 2, 1842–1848.*

Thorson, Robert M. *Walden's Shore: Henry David Thoreau and Nineteenth-Century Science.* Cambridge, Mass.: Harvard University Press, 2014.

Venter, Craig. *Life at the Speed of Light: From the Double Helix to the Dawn of Digital Life.* New York: Penguin, 2013.

Virilio, Paul. *Open Sky.* Translated by Julie Rose. New York: Verso, 1997.

Walls, Laura Dassow. *Henry David Thoreau: A Life.* Chicago: University of Chicago Press, 2017.

———. *Seeing New Worlds: Henry David Thoreau and Nineteenth-Century Natural Science.* Madison: University of Wisconsin Press, 1995.

Warn, Dana. "Artists Change Scientists' Perspectives." ABC News, August 21, 2000. http://www.abcnews.go.com/Technology/story?id=120020&page=1.

Wilkins, Thurman. *Thomas Moran: Artist of the Mountains.* Norman: University of Oklahoma Press, 1966.

Willis, Nathaniel P. *American Scenery; or, Land, Lake, and River: Illustrations of Transatlantic Nature.* 2 vols. London: George Virtue, 1840.

Wilson, Edward O. "Biophilia and the Conservation Ethic." In *The Biophilia Hypothesis*, edited by Stephen R. Kellert and Edward O. Wilson, 31–40. Washington, D.C.: Shearwater Books, 1993.

———. *Biophilia: The Human Bond with Other Species.* Cambridge, Mass.: Harvard University Press, 1984.

———. *The Future of Life.* New York: Vintage, 2002.

———. *The Meaning of Human Existence.* New York: Liveright, 2014.

Wilson, Leslie Perrin. "Walden: Pilgrimages and Iconographies." In *The Oxford Book of Transcendentalism*, edited by Joel Myerson, Sandra Harbert Petrulionis, and Laura Dassow Walls, 659–70. New York: Oxford University Press, 2010.

Winthrop, John. "A Modell of Christian Charity." In *The Founding of Massachusetts: Historians and the Sources*, edited by Edmund S. Morgan, 190–204. Indianapolis, Ind.: Bobbs-Merrill, 1964.

Wittgenstein, Ludwig. *Philosophical Investigations*. Edited by G. E. M. Anscombe and R. Rhees, translated by G. E. M. Anscombe. Oxford, U.K.: Blackwell, 1963.

Woolf, Virginia. "Thoreau." In *The Essays of Virginia Woolf*, vol. 2, edited by Andrew McNeillie, 132–40. San Diego, Calif.: Harcourt Brace Jovanovich, 1987.

Wordsworth, William. "Preface to *Lyrical Ballads*." In *Wordsworth and Coleridge: Lyrical Ballads and Other Poems*, edited by Martin P. Scofield, 5–25. Ware, Hertfordshire, U.K.: Wordsworth Editions, 2003.

INDEX

and fully engineered landscape, 97, 105, 121, 133; and improvement of nature, 47, 54, 55, 96, 98–99, 100, 103, 114–15, 118–20, 121–22; and "Island Civilization" (Nash), 121–22; nineteenth-century views of, 97, 98–99, 114–15, 116, 117, 118–19, 120–21, 122, 144; and *Sierra Club v. Morton*, 122–24; Thoreau and, 2, 5, 26, 40, 41, 98, 115–16, 117–19, 123–24, 125–29, 134, 144; and Yosemite National Park, 120–21, 122, 144. *See also* Concord: as benign environment

Euler, Leonard, 42

Fair Haven Hill, 2, 43
Faulkner, William, 24
fields and meadows, 8, 24, 25, 36, 41, 48, 53, 55, 79, 84, 92, 93, 100, 102, 103, 104, 105, 109, 110, 111, 114, 115, 119, 138
Fitchburg Railroad, 1, 3, 101, 135, 141, 142
Flaubert, Gustave, 13, 28, 29, 31, 37
Foster, David R., 110
Franzen, Jonathan, 5
Frémont, John, 52–53, 54, 72
Fromm, Erich, 125
Frost, Robert, 16
Fuller, Margaret, 17, 71, 72

Gabo, Naum, 117
Gama, Vasco de, 12
Gell-Mann, Murray, 18
Gleason, Herbert Wendell, 3, 64, 74, 86, 106, 136
Godard, Jean-Luc, 51, 59, 60
Goethe, Johann Wolfgang von, 19, 49, 66, 81, 82, 93
Goldsmith, Kenneth, 19, 28, 141
Goncourt, Edmund de, 44
Goncourt, Jules de, 44
Goose Pond, 43, 56
Gould, Stephen J., 83
Gowing's Swamp, 29, 85–86, 88–89, 101, 103, 110, 117
Grape Cliff Cardinal Ditch, 84

Great Meadow, 92
Griswold, Rufus Wilmot, 52

Haacke, Hans, 139
Harding, Walter, 11
Hawthorne, Nathaniel, 11, 14, 76
Hawthorne, Sophia, 11
Heidegger, Martin, 119
Heizer, Michael, 95, 136, 138, 141; *Double Negative*, 130–35, 143, 144
Hemingway, Ernest, 27
Hesiod, 54
Heywood's Meadow, 53
Hobbes, Thomas, 80
Hoffman, Abbie, 5
Holt, Nancy, 95
Hopper, Edward, 10
Hosmer, Alfred Winslow, 38
Hosmer, Edmund, 43
House, Patrick, 140
Houston, Sam, 4
Hubbard's Swamp, 84
Hudson River, 34, 95, 99, 108
Humboldt, Alexander von, 114

Indian removal, 4, 79, 128
Inness, George, 54

Jackson, William H., 73
Jamieson, Dale, 126, 134
Jefferson, Thomas, 36, 128
Johnson, Lyndon Baines, 124, 125–26
Johnson, Samuel, 27, 53
July Fourth, 26, 36

Kac, Eduardo, 140
Kafka, Franz, 27, 30
Kant, Immanuel, 11, 113–14, 116–17, 123, 127
Kateb, George, 159
Kauffman, Stuart A., and "adjacent possible," 108–9, 111
Kazin, Alfred, 35
Keats, John, 31, 36, 48, 102
Kibbe Place Swamp, 84